Unchained

First Edition

Print edition ISBN: 9781631113987

Copyright © Stacey Chatman 2017

This is a work of creative nonfiction. The events are portrayed to the best of Stacey Chatman's memory. While all stories in this book are true, names and identifying details have been changed to protect the privacy of the people involved.

Printed with BAM! Publishing diy.bampublish.com

Unchained - Co-Dependency

Unchained

A Woman's Struggle With Co-Dependency to Gain

Self-Worth

Stacey Chatman

Matthew Lofton

Doug Swaim

Diane Jones

Alan Rathburn

Published by BAM! Publishing

Table of Contents

Disclaimer

This is a work of creative nonfiction. The events are portrayed to the best of Stacey Chatman's memory. While all stories in this book are true, names and identifying details have been changed to protect the privacy of the people involved.

Preface

I believe in life we are given challenges and obstacles to strengthen us, not to weaken us! My overcoming challenges has allowed me to not remain a victim but to survive and by surviving I have learned to "Rise above the Tide"

~ Stacey Chatman~

Introduction

"Mom, please, please, don't put me on that bus. Please, I promise to be a good girl!. I promise to be a good girl, like my sister," I promised, as I stood looking my mother in her dark brown eyes"

No Place To Call Home

.

At the age of 17, my Mom asked me what I wanted to do with my life. I told her I wanted to go to college. She said "Stacey, we don't have the money for that." I said, "Don't worry about it, I'll figure it out." My Mom asked me why I did not want to go into the military like my twin sister. She stated how much easier it would be, especially financially. I said, perhaps a bit defiantly, "Mom, I do not think I am the military type, you know I will tell the drill-sergeant what he could do with the push-up!"

Regardless of my mother's adamant tone and piercing eyes, I made the decision not to join the military. I knew perhaps she wanted the best for me. She simply could not come up with the best solution to support me financially. She was a single mother raising twin daughters and did not have the finances to support me while attending college.

Throughout our lives, my mother relied on the support of my grandparents to assist raising my sister and I. When growing up, my sister and I did not see our father much. In fact, we were not told who our biological father was until we were eight years old. I still remember the confused look on our faces when our mother told us. My sister and I thought my mother's long-term boyfriend, Lorenzo, was our father. Lorenzo assisted my mother with raising us until we were six years old.

My sister and I were born three months premature; we only weighed 3 lbs. when we were born. We were hospitalized for three months. Nine months prior to our coming into this world my mother and father, child-hood friends, were at a party and "hooked-up". They partied that evening and we were conceived. Shortly thereafter my mother moved to New York and my father went back to his military station. My mother was informed she was pregnant and she stayed in New York until it was time for her to give birth. When giving birth, my mother had no idea she was going to give birth to twin daughters. My father was not there. My maternal grandparents supported my mother while raising my sister and I. At times, we lived with our grandparents and then our mother. My grandparents lived very close to us. Our living situation remained like this until we graduated high school .

My mom's solution to the college problem was to sign me up for a government program without my permission. This program would allow me to attend college for 2 years, but first I had to fulfill the necessary requirements of taking college preparation classes and passing the ACT Exam. It would take 3 months for me to fulfill these requirements.

I remember getting on that bus in Lewistown, Pennsylvania with only $40 dollars in my pocket. I was so afraid. As I sat in my seat, I slowly slid my body closer to the guy sitting next to me. I wanted to feel the warmth of his body. I did not want to feel alone.

When I arrived at the Job Corps Center in Charleston, West Virginia, it was not what I expected. I walked into the inner-city for the first time! When I walked into the gray, outdated building, on one side there were girls looking at me and they would say "If you look at my man, I will kick your ass." On the other side, there were guys in the corner saying. "Come here shorty, I might just want to tap that ass." I was scared and frightened. I just kept moving my feet forward. I glanced around looked at the gray walls and wondered, "What in the Hell is this?" I tried to settle in, I just went along with the flow and did as I was told from the counselors that I was assigned. I arrived on a Tuesday at the Job Corps Center in Charleston, West Virginia.

Each Tuesday or Wednesday new recruits would arrive at the Job Corps Center. Students arriving were either learning a technical skill or preparing to go to college. Upon arriving, I was provided with my roommate assignments, which consisted of three roommates. I was given clothing vouchers and a stipend. It was completely frightening for a 17 year old girl. For the first time I felt like I had no place to call home. I was alone and isolated from everything that I knew and loved. I adhered to the schedule that was brought to me by the counselors. I had no other choice. Once I got settled into my dorm room, it was time to eat dinner. During the cafeteria style dinner, I laid eyes on and darted toward the first white girl I saw. This girl had thick bottle cap glasses, dirty blond hair, a nervous crooked smile and she wore clothes that were possibly one or two sizes too small. I thought to myself, "There is no way in hell this white girl will harm me." In an instant, I felt safe. So I darted as quickly as I could toward her. I sat next to her and asked her what her name was. She said, "Rayelynn", with a deep West Virginian accent. I said, "Where are you from?" She said, "I'm from up the holla." I giggled, "What is a holla?" She said, "That is what we West Virginians call a road." She started talking about the flowers and trees that sat along the "holla", with excitement I thought "Hot damn she is talking my language." Rayelynn and I had something in common we were both country girls. Instantly, we felt a connection that would help us get through the chaos set before us. Rayelynn and I sat and looked at the confusion in the room. The room was full of teenagers that knew the street life, some were joking with each other, some were arguing, and other looked as lost as me and Rayelynn.

A young man approached us and introduced himself. He said we looked scared and he wanted to "protect" us. This young man introduced himself as Marco. Marco was 5'6", dark-skinned, nicely built. Marco seemed to maneuver through the chaos with ease and grace. When I asked where he was from, he stated Pittsburgh, Pennsylvania. Since Marco was from Pittsburgh, this easily explained why the chaos did not appear to startle him. Marco stated that Rayelynn and I looked like frightened rabbits and we both shook our heads with agreement.

Marco said with certainty that we should not worry, that he would look out for us. From then on, the three of us ate breakfast, lunch, and dinner together. We also hung out during free time. After three months, the three of us transferred to the college campus. We were accepted to the West Virginia Institute of Technology in Montgomery, West Virginia. I chose to study legal administration. I had hopes of becoming an attorney. Rayelynn and I became college roommates. Marco and I began dating.

The college campus was an exciting change and Marco and I were inseparable. One day Marco asked for the IT, my eyes became huge! The IT was something a girl does not give away. When I was a little girl, my sister and I would play with all the kids in our neighborhood. Always around nightfall my sister and I could hear my grandmother's voice "twins, bring your asses home." I just adored my grandmother because she was a tell it like a "tell it like it is type of woman. When we got home, she would look at us square in the eyes and said. "I seen ya playing with those little boys. Did they ask for the IT?" We would shake our heads and say no grandma, they did not ask for the IT. She would say, well good and you better not give IT away because that is ALL they want and once they get the IT, they will leave or they will give you more problems to deal with! Then she would say, "I better not ever hear about you giving IT away and you better keep your legs closed! Do you understand?" My sister and I shook our heads, "Yes, ma'am!"

When Marco asked for IT, I said, "No thank you," while crossing my legs awkwardly but saying politely with an awkward smile, "I am sorry I want to wait until I'm married to give IT away." Marco seemed to understand.

On Friday's, our college campus became deserted. Some kids went home for the weekend and some kids simply partied. Marco and I hung out in our dorm rooms and ate pizza, this was our norm. One Friday, I went to Marco's dorm room, and we ordered pizza, we studied and played music. He looked at me and asked me to sit on the bed next to him. He had his text book in his hand, he said he wanted to show me what he was studying. After he showed me his chemistry formulas and tried to explain to me what he was studying, we began kissing. All of sudden he held me so tight that I could not move. He forcefully laid me down on the bed. The next thing I knew he was on top of me. He forced my zipper open and pulled my pants down, he placed his hands on top of my mouth so I could not yell. I struggled! He was overpowering me, he pried my legs apart and forced his dick in me. I remember closing my eyes not believing what was happening. I was so confused. He pleasured himself and then he sat upright. I sat up and cried. I was shocked and confused and ashamed. He took my "IT" and then I remembered thinking, I will make this work. I remembered the promise I made to myself that I would marry the person that I lost my virginity.

I was "Date Raped", no voice, no power, no family near. I was full of confusion! A virgin and my IT was gone! I was confused about the entire experience. I told myself "well I am dating him, so it was ok." Because of my beliefs, I would remain with Marco. I was determined that I would marry the man that I lost my virginity. I was a good Christian girl and I listened very well to my grandmother.

As the weeks went on, I became depressed. I remembered taking walks on campus. The campus had wonderful scenic views of the West Virginia Appalachian Mountains. Although their gorgeous appearance would brighten anyone's day, I would stare at the mountains and sob. I was going through a transformational time in my life without any moral and emotional support.

I Stayed

Despite my confused feelings, I remained in the relationship with Marco. My main reason, he got my IT. My IT was important to me because my grandmother told me to protect it. She told me a girl should cherish her IT. I spent my teenage years protecting my IT. My boyfriends tried to ask for the IT. Once they asked for the IT, we were no longer dating. My IT became a teenage topic of discussion.I was called the last virgin of Mount Union.I did not care. I brushed it off and kept it moving.I was proud to be a virgin. Marco got my IT, therefore, I stayed!

I shifted my focus on college. My main goal was to get my associate degree in Legal Administration. Marco's goal was to become a pharmacist. He studied Chemistry. For two years. we both studied diligently. I received my associate degree in Legal Administration. Marco received his associate degree in chemistry. We moved to Woodbridge, Virginia. We stayed with my Aunt, Mia. I began working as a Patent Law legal secretary in Arlington, Virginia. Marco transferred to Howard University. Marco needed to complete his bachelors degree.

Marco and I placed a deposit on our first apartment. With excitement, we arrived at the rental office to pick up keys to the apartment. Upon our arrival, the excitement quickly diminished when the staff informed us the apartment was no longer available. Marco and I left disappointed. I looked in his eyes and could see he was angry. I tried to console him. All of a sudden, he raised his hand and slapped me across the face. I was stunned! I remembered looking at the highway behind me. The cars were heading toward the Pentagon .I looked back at him. He just stared at me.His facial expression remained the same.He showed no remorse. I was hurt and confused.

We moved back in with my Aunt Mia. Three weeks later, we were able to find a one bedroom apartment in Alexandria, Virginia. The apartment was approximately two miles from the first apartment. The apartment was beautiful. It had hard wood floors, a nice sized living and dining room area, separate kitchen, bathroom and bedroom.

I thought the slap across the face was an isolated incident. One day, I arranged a lunch date with my cousin, Dawn. She also lived in Alexandria. Before my leaving for lunch, Marco inspected my clothes. He told me to change my shirt. I was wearing a white T-Shirt and shorts. After he went to go study, I decided to wear what I had on and not change my shirt. After my lunch date, Marco surprisingly met me at the bus stop. He saw that I was wearing the t-shirt that he had forbidden me to wear. We got on the bus. He gently pushed me up against the window. He whispered in my ear. He said; "Wait until we get home."When we got home, he slapped me across the face. I ran from one end of the apartment to the other end with no escape. He raped me! After he raped me, I stood in front of him crying. He gently touched me and said; "sorry."He asked me to give him a blow job. Forcefully, he held my head, I placed one knee at a time down on the hardwood floor. He opened his legs. He enjoyed it! I thought it was disgusting! Tears flowed from my eyes. All I could think about is "how will I get out of this?"

After the beatings and rapes, I felt alone and isolated. I could not share what I was going through with anyone.I felt my mother betrayed me. My sister did not need to hear my pain. She joined the military and was in Europe.

The longer I did not fight back the more I endured. One evening, Marco made me sit in between his legs as we watched television. .He held a carpet cutter up against my throat. For thirty minutes, he told me not to move. I shivered and I did not move! I had no control over the outcome. I just breathed slowly and pretended to watch T.V. After the Cosby show, he asked me to make him dinner. As tears rolled down my face, he apologized. He came and caressed me and asked me not to cry.I said to him; "You are the one making me cry".That evening I wallowed in my tears, feeling alone.

An abuser always knows how to weaken you. The rapes, the beatings, the sodomy were not enough. One evening he turned off the light. I was dragged into the bathroom. We both stood in between the toilet and bathtub. He held my head tightly. He told me that he would cut off my breasts if I did not obey him.

The thoughts of leaving were my everyday daydream. But then I would hear Marco's voice inside my head. Marco would often share with me how his sister was murdered by her boyfriend.She was stabbed 26 times. Her fiancé thought she was cheating on him. Her murder changed his entire family's outlook on life.

Marco's family valued him.They knew he would be the most successful. Marco, just like myself, was considered a disadvantaged youth. He joined the Job Corps to get his associate degree. Marco was raised by a single mother. She was on welfare. He grew up in the projects of Pittsburgh. He called the projects "The Hill".The Hill is considered one of the toughest parts of Pittsburgh. Marco survived the streets. Marco sent money home to help his family. When we
would visit his family, he would buy food for them. While visiting his family, Marco and I would
often visit his mentor. He owned a pharmacy. Marco would talk about his first job. He was grateful for having a father figure. Marco could easily charm people. He had strong work ethics. He had a sense of humor. He was a dedicated employee and friend. While Marco displayed great characteristics, I experienced Marco's dark, controlling, intense, vicious, demeaning, and dangerous sides.

Beginning To Transition

I wanted to forget the secret I was hiding. I concentrated on my career. Being a legal secretary at a patent law firm became boring. I began searching for another job. I interviewed for a secretarial position at the George Mason University School of Law in Arlington, Virginia.I was ecstatic when I got the job.The transition was welcomed and I enjoyed being in an environment where higher learning was the ultimate achievement.

One day, while answering the phones, I was introduced to David Johnson. David was an incoming Law Student. When I looked at David, I was immediately attracted to his good looks, confidence, and intelligence. David was the Lenny Kravitz of GMU Law School. He made it very "cool" to be a law student. David was sexy as hell and he certainly had my attention. David's smooth smile would make any woman's heart melt. David displayed charm, confidence, and grace easily. I wanted those qualities.

I needed to get to know him. David would frequently visit my desk and say hello and we would engage in light conversation. During one of our conversations, David asked if I had a boyfriend and I told him yes. David's response was "That is too bad, there are lots of guys in this school that would like to get to know you, including myself." I was flattered and I wanted to get to know him too!

Each week, David would stop by my desk to say hello. I would always respond; "I'm fine." One afternoon , David asked how I was doing and I responded by saying, "I'm not doing very well today" He said, "If you ever want to talk about it, let me know." I said, "ok!"The next day David stopped by my desk and said, "Are you ready to talk about it? I said, "yes!" I let him know the secret I was hiding. He looked at me and said "You are the one that has to make the change; how long are you going to put up with it?" He was to the point! He was right!

The following weekend, Marco was away and I was in the apartment alone. There was nothing but me and silence. I heard the whisper of God speak to me. God's whisper said, "You must get out of this." I answered; "how?" "Marco is all I have ever known!" I asked God " What is was going to be like to leave Marco?" I closed my eyes and heard the following. "You have such a wonderful life ahead of you, but if you remain in this relationship one day he will kill you! When you leave, it is not going to be easy. It will feel like you are drowning, you will go up and you will go down, but in the end you will land on a rock". In my heart, at that moment, I decided to leave Marco.

The following week, my cousin Dawn called and asked me if Marco and I wanted to join her and her boyfriend on a double date in Washington, D.C. Throughout the week, we made plans for Friday evening. When Friday approached, Marco stated he had to study and he would not be able to go. He told me it was ok if I continued on with the plans without him.

Dawn arrived at the apartment around 7 pm and we began speaking about the plans for the evening. Marco listened intently as he would occasionaly glance up from his book. All of a sudden he said "Stacey you're not going!". I looked at him and said, "Yes, I am going Dawn and I made plans all week and I am going!". Marco got up from his seat and approached me and said "You need to come into the bedroom." He stormed into the bedroom. I looked at my cousin and said "Dawn, whatever you do, please do not leave me." She nodded.

When I went into the room, he said "So you are showing off in front of your cousin, uh?" I said "No!, I am upset because I made plans all week and now they are ruined". He said, "Well, I don't want you to go and I said I want to go". He said, "OK!" After the conversation, we both walked down the hall toward the living room. The room was silent, my cousin left. I felt empty inside. I turned quickly to look at Marco; he had the glare in his eyes. Quickly, he grabbed me and dragged me back into the bedroom. He slammed the door and began slapping me across the face. The tears, combined with the pressure of his force just made me close my eyes and struggle.

After he stopped beating me, he looked at me and said, "you know I love you." I was silent. He sat up on the side of the bed and said "Get up and suck my dick." I slowly got up and walked over to him. I placed each knee down on the floor. He opened his legs and I did as instructed with tears flowing down my face. After that, he raped me.

The Morning After

Early the next morning, Dawn called me to see how I was doing. I told her that she should not have left me. I told her that Marco raped and beat me. Dawn asked me if I wanted to go to Pennsylvania and visit my mother. I said, yes. I told Marco I was going home to see my mother. He gave me a blank stare. I packed an overnight bag and when my cousin arrived, I left.

During the 3 hour drive, I was quiet. Dawn talked about her evening with her boyfriend. I listened. All I could think about was the beating, sodomy, and rape I had endured. When we got to my mother's home, Dawn and I discussed a time for her to pick me up the next day. I grabbed my bags and went into the house.

I was excited to see my mother and step-father simply being normal. My mother was cleaning and cooking.My step-father was watching T.V. I said; "hello" and sat on the couch.They each asked how I was doing and I said' "fine". I did not say a lot, just watched T.V. and engaged in light conversation. Frequently, I would get up and walk into my bedroom and lie on the bed and rest.

That evening at dinner, my step-father looked at me and said; "Stacey, what happened to your lip?" I said, "Oh, I accidently hit myself" .He looked away and finished his meal.

After dinner I went to visit my grandmother. Her health was declining. I sat and talked with her about anything she wanted to talk about. She spoke about what she wanted to accomplish in life and how she felt held back. She often spoke to me about not achieving any of her goals in life. My grandmother could sing, dance, cook, and spoke fluent French. She told me her greatest accomplishment was raising kids; however her facial expression showed disappointment, not a sense of accomplishment.

After visiting with my grandmother, I went back home and watched a movie with my mother and step-father and went to bed. The next morning, I was quiet, ate breakfast, relaxed, and early that afternoon, Dawn picked me up and we were back on the road to Virginia. Before leaving, I promised my mother that I would call once I arrived home.

As promised, once I arrived home, I called home. When my mother answered the phone, I told her I made it home safely. My mother said, "Stacey, I want to ask you something." I said, "ok." She said, "Is Marco beating you?" I could not speak. My mother said; "George, said he noticed your lip and knew that you were being beat." My mother asked, "How long has this been going on?" I said "two years." She said, we have to get you out of there.I said' "how?" She said, "I will call your Aunt Mia and I will be in touch."

The next morning, my aunt contacted me and asked me if the physical abuse was true.I told her; "yes!" She said, "Your mother wants you out of this!" My aunt asked; "Why did you not tell anyone?" I said, "Because I did not trust anyone".My aunt, got quiet and said, "By the end of the weekend, you will have to come live with me." I said; "ok!" I broke down in tears.

Marco was going to be attending a study session at Howard University for most of the upcoming weekend. During the week, I planned with my aunt, the belongings I would take. Saturday morning came, my demeanor was normal to Marco. Before he left the apartment, he grabbed my arm and said; "if you should leave this apartment to even take out the garbage, I will beat you when I return!" Once he left, I called my aunt! She was there within an hour! We loaded the van with the belongings and I was gone! I cried, sobbed and wept all the way to Woodbridge.

The next day, I received a call from Marco and his voice was shaken.He said; "I can't believe you did this to us?" He said; "I will make it work for us." I said; "ok!" He said; "I would like to see you one last time." I said, "ok. I can arrange a visit within the next week with my family waiting outside. He said; "ok." We hung up and I sobbed.

The Visit

The following Saturday, I met Marco at the apartment. When I walked into the living room, there was no furniture. At that moment, I realized, for the first time, he was hurting. I stood there looking at him. He was playing music. I will never forget these two songs. "A House is Not a Home" by Luther Vandross and "Cause I Love You" by Lynnie Williams. Every time I hear the song "Cause I Love you" I cry and my facial expression becomes blank! This is PTSD at its best. There are some things that will always have an everlasting impression on my spirit, my mind and my SOUL! I left him sitting alone in the empty apartment.

I have spent a lifetime healing from this relationship. As I look back on my childhood, my sister and I witnessed, on numerous occasions domestic abuse. My mother was physically abused in front of us.

My sister and I thought my mother's long-term boyfriend, Lyle, was our biological father. Tracey and I loved Lyle. Lyle bought us our first pets. Those dogs drove my mother crazy. Lyle would sit us on his lap and hug us like a dad should.

My mother and Lyle struggled to continue to keep a healthy relationship. My mother and Lyle would argue in front of us. I remember my mother saying; "They think that you are their dad?" He would look at her. Then, he would look and us, and he decided to stay.

One night, my mother and Lyle got in a physical fight. There was yelling! He took a telephone cord and wrapped it around my mother's neck! My sister and I ran towards our mother; as we held onto her, the scuffle continued. All of a sudden, I broke loose and my sister still held onto our mother. As the struggle continued, all of a sudden, there was a crash and then silence! The crash, in the struggle, was the china cabinet. It fell on my sister! She was covered in glass! Her eyes were closed. My mother screamed! I remember the chaos. My sister began to cry .Lyle and my mother began picking up the pieces of glass away from my sister.She was checked to make sure she was not bleeding. I remember my mother and Lyle being happy she was not hurt, no bleeding. Lyle and my mother both helped my sister. Scared and frightened, I watched!

My mother placed the phone back on the receiver and she called my grandparents. My grandparents arrived. There was a heated argument! After the argument, Lyle packed his bags and left.

My childhood saviors were my grandparents, Margie and Paul. Margie and Paul were an interesting couple. They loved, despised, and hated each other. Monday through Thursday Margie and Paul engaged in their normal routines; however on Friday hell broke loose! The drinking binges occurred. I refer to these binges as getting into the spirits. On the weekends, it was normal, to see my grandmother go into a rage about her life. It was normal to see my grandfather say very little. On Friday and Saturday, it was normal for the dark and white liquors (the spirits) to take control. It was normal to watch Margie and Paul engage in a marriage mixed with love, resentment and hatred. On the weekends, it was normal for family to have dinner and when the spirits were in control; all of a sudden my grandmother would slap my grandfather so hard that he would fall to the floor; he was drunk. He would stumble back to his chair, place his hat back on his head, look at me and my sister and look away. Sometimes he would stare at us blankly drunk and sometimes he would let a tear flow from his eyes. Equally, I loved Margie and Paul, no judgment, I just observed.

The Transition

I stayed at my Aunt Mia's house for about a month. I did not own a car and the daily commute from Woodbridge to Arlington became difficult. My cousin, Dawn and I became roommates and rented an apartment in Alexandria, Virginia. I focused on work and rebuilding my life without Marco.

While at work, Dave Johnson, The Lenny Kravitz of GMU Law School, would stop by my desk to see how I was doing. He noticed I had difficulty adjusting to the transition. One day he asked me out on a date. I was flattered. We went to dinner near the Boston Mall in Arlington, VA. It was the Christmas Holiday Season. After dinner, we choose to go inside the mall and window shop. As we stopped and glanced at the Christmas decorations, we glanced at each other, his eyes stared into mine and he leaned towards me and his lips touched mine. My heart began to beat so FAST! He was so damn FINE!

After the date, Dave and I began seeing each other more frequently. After he would get finished with his classes, he would stop by the apartment. I would de-stress him by giving him a massage. I would ask him if he had dinner. If not, I would make him dinner. Sometimes Dave was too tired to drive home so he would study at my apartment. Dave would share with me the pressures of being a Law Student. Dave was Vice President of the BLSA, Black Law Student Association. In addition to studying, he was responsible for organizing student events. I was addicted to him. I was always marveled by Dave's eyes. His eyes illuminated determination, persistence, success, and boldness. Dave had an unstoppable presence and energy about him. I wanted what he had and I did not know how to get it! I was jealous of him. This jealousy caused us to have a love – hate type of relationship that evolved around great sex.

After he was finished studying, we would go to my room and have the most passionate sex; the all night long type of sex that would have me yearning for more. This type of sex made me late for work and made him late for school. Damn! IT was Good! I was addicted to him!

Dave's family dynamics were different than mine. Dave had a nuclear family in which there was much support emotionally and financially. Dave's parents supported him financially while he studied Spanish at William and Mary in Williamsburg, Va. After he received his Undergraduate degree Dave enrolled in The George Mason University School of Law. I was also envious that Dave had a family that supported his educational endeavors. These were moments that I felt like I was at a disadvantage from other people that had a supportive environment.

.

Alone Again

Dave introduced me to his parents and me and Dave's mother, May had something in common she was born and raised in Central City, Kentucky. Central City is a coal miners town. May would share with me her experiences growing up and I would listen and reminisce about my country girl up bringing. May and I bonded. Dave's father was a government employee. Dave's parents were established. I admired them.

Dave and I would often have Sunday dinners with his mother and father. I enjoyed these Sunday dinners I felt connected to a family.

Dave and I dated the entire time he was in Law School. Dave always challenged me in areas of professional and self-development. At times, we would argue, because I felt he was being over critical of me. I was stuck in the mind-set of working, paying bills and starting a family. I was not focused on self-development.

Dave and I always had great intimacy; however we did not relate in the areas of professional growth. I was not progressing as quickly in this area that he would have liked. I felt like I had a lot of catching up to do and I was insecure. We would often argue about my areas of growth and Dave was not faithful in our relationship.

I attended Dave's Law School Graduation party. We celebrated with his friends and colleagues. That night, Dave and I made love. I told him that I see myself being the next Mrs. Johnson. After we made love, Dave told me that he had to tell me something. I looked at him and he said: "Stacey, I want you to know that I will always love and share something special with you." I said; "ok." He said, "I am getting married!" I was furious! I said; "How can you make love to me one minute and tell me you're getting married the next minute?" I told him; "Don't ever speak to me again! If you even think about contacting me again, think twice about it and don't do it!"

I was heart broken; I lost my best-friend and I lost my relationship with May a woman I referred to as Mom. Once again, I felt lost and displaced in this world. After the break up with Dave, I became very reflective about my life, about my future and where I saw myself professionally.

My continuing to work at George Mason University School of Law provided me with constant memories of Dave and my relationship! I began searching for a new job and I became an administrative assistant at a Patent Law Firm in Crystal City, VA. I did not like the atmosphere of this job and I knew immediately I would transition soon.

I would sit and think about the many conversations Dave and I had about my returning to college to work towards a bachelors degree. I began researching universities and I decided to go to VCU, Virginia Commonwealth University, in Richmond, VA.

In order to save money, I got a second job as a hotel operator at the Marriott in Crystal City. I primarily worked on the weekends. I told my mother that I was accepted to attend VCU and she said she did not support my decision of quitting my job and moving to Richmond. I applied for financial aid and enrolled in residential housing. That August, I ,moved to Richmond. I took with me determination that I would earn a bachelors degree.

Once I arrived in Richmond, I was excited about the future. I received a small grant to assist with college expenses. I got a part-time job working as an operator in a hotel. I enrolled in 15 credit hours of classes, which consisted of general education requirements; I did not decide on a major. I enjoyed being in the college atmosphere again. One of the classes I enrolled was Italian Foreign Language Studies. I was very focused and determined to make excellent grades but I was having difficulty with learning Italian. I made an appointment to get help from my professor. He eagerly assisted me and I was grateful for the help. Overall, my areas of studies were going well.

I was working hard at my part-time job and studying. I did not have time to focus on friendships, therefore, I just focused on my goals. My mother would check on me frequently. She let me know that my grandmother's health was declining rapidly. My grandmother was diagnosed with cancer, ten years prior. I would call my grandmother and talk with her. When I did not have to work on weekends, I would go home and visit her. We would sit and talk about her life. She would speak about her joys, singing, dancing. My grandmother would always become sad when she spoke about the unfinished dreams. When she talked about these unfinished dreams, the light in her eyes dimmed. The conversation would often lead into the disappointment of a difficult marriage, in which she felt trapped. At the end of her life, she felt her only purpose was to raise kids, grandchildren, upkeep the home. I felt her resentment towards my grandfather and I felt her sorrow for the dreams that will never come to fruition.

After my visits with my grandmother, I made a commitment to myself that I would never let a man keep me from achieving any goal, aspiration or dream that I had for myself. I promised Only God and me would have ultimate control of my destiny.

When I returned to school, I tried to remain focused on studies. I would often seek assistance from my foreign language professor. One day I went to his office he leaned over and kissed me. He told me, "Stacey, you are Motta Bella and I would like you to be my mistress". I was stunned, I did not know how to react, so I did not react. I did not frequent his office after that. It seems after that incident everything at VCU began to unravel! I was not as focused as I was a few short months prior. I was struggling financially and I did not know if I would be able to complete the full year! Spiritually, I felt like I needed to be closer to God. In between classes, I would frequent a Catholic Church near the campus and get on my knees and cry my heart to God. I would ask God for guidance with my life. I was actually considering taking my professor up on his option. I stopped by my professor's office and spoke to him about it. He told me he had a room in the back of his home and that he would financially assist me. This offer sounded good, but my heart and soul were heavy.

In the morning, while I was getting ready for college, I began listening to the evangelist, Marilyn Hickey. I enjoyed her simplistic spiritual messages. I was still going to the Catholic Church and would bow down on my knees and pray about my future. On one occasion, I spoke to a priest about my uneasiness about my future and he prayed with me.

At the end of the day, I found myself mentally, emotionally and spiritually exhausted. When I would return to my apartment, I spoke to my roommates regarding my financial pressures and let them know that I did not know if I would be able to complete the school year.

One evening, I went to bed early and fell into a deep sleep. During the night, I began to wrestle in my sleep. All of a sudden, I gasped for a single breath, I sprung straight up in my bed, my heart was pounding! At that moment, I knew my beloved Grandmother Margie, died. I felt her spirit transition from this world. One hour later, my mother called to officially tell me something that my soul already knew.

It Is Well With Her Soul

My precious Grandmother, Margie was gone. The strong vibrant woman whose spirit was larger than life was no longer present on this earth. The family matriarch would not be accessible to seek advice and guidance.

Memories of her flooded my mind. The last words that she told me still resonate with me. When visiting her the last time, I walked into her bedroom. She laid there frail. She was reaching for her medical marijuana. I stood at the foot of her bed and began to cry. She struggled to sit up in her bed. Once she sat upright, she pointed her finger and glared at me. She looked me in the eyes and said "Get Out, Get Out of this room. Don't cry for me, because IT is Well with my soul!" She said, "Leave this room and when your done crying come back in here." I left sobbing.

I stood in the hallway and cried and wiped tears away! When I was finally done crying, I walked back in the room and she still was sitting upright. She said to me, "Are you done crying for me?" I said; "yes"! She repeated; "It is well with my soul!" She then said; "Stacey, in life, I never want you to become despondent. Do you understand me?" I said, "yes!" Because of those powerful words, I always carry hope in my heart and I always share messages of hope and faith.

Mistress or College Dropout

I returned to Richmond feeling a great sense of loss and grief. I tried to get back on track with studying and work. I felt the financial pressure. When I went to college in West Virginia, I only had to focus on studies, not juggling work at the same time. It was challenging.

I began contemplating the withdrawal of college and moving back to Northern Virginia. I got information on how to withdrawal from school. One of my roommates mother offered to assist me financially and I politely declined. I spoke to my professor about his offer, I was considering it.

I continued to watch Marilyn Hickey in the morning to find the answers I needed. I continued to go the Catholic Church and get on my knees and pour my heart out to God. One afternoon, while my roommates were at classes, I picked up my Bible and said; "God, I am really struggling. God I am going to open up my bible and I need you to speak to me right now!" I closed my eyes tightly, I was desperate for the answer. I opened my eyes and gently rubbed the Bible. Suddenly, I flipped the Bible open and the scripture I read was Matthew 6 versus 25-34

Do Not Worry:
25 "Therefore I tell you, do not worry about your life, what you will eat or drink; or about your body, what you will wear. Is not life more than food, and the body more than clothes? 26 Look at the birds of the air; they do not sow or reap or store away in barns, and yet your heavenly Father feeds them. Are you not much more valuable than they?27 Can any one of you by worrying add a single hour to your life[a]?

28 "And why do you worry about clothes? See how the flowers of the field grow. They do not labor or spin. 29 Yet I tell you that not even Solomon in all his splendor was dressed like one of these. 30 If that is how God clothes the grass of the field, which is here today and tomorrow is thrown into the fire, will he not much more clothe you—you of little faith? 31 So do not worry, saying, 'What shall we eat?' or 'What shall we drink?' or 'What shall we wear?' 32 For the pagans run after all these things, and your heavenly Father knows that you need them.33 But seek first his kingdom and his righteousness, and all these things will be given to you as well. 34 Therefore do not worry about tomorrow, for tomorrow will worry about itself. Each day has enough trouble of its own. "

I knew what I needed to do and I needed to withdraw from college and move back to Northern Virginia and find a job. I withdrew from school before my academic records could be affected. I was scared, I had to find a job. I moved back in with my aunt Mia In Woodbridge.

Unleashed Faith

I understood that I should not worry about how I was going to make it! God was going to look out for me just as he looks out for the fowls in the air. He provides food for creatures. I understood that I should not worry about my clothing, God was going to look out for me. I felt a huge burden lift off my shoulders because I knew what direction I should go! The decision was made. I unleashed my faith that my survival was in God's hands.

I was living on unleashed faith and about $500 in my pocket. I had joy in my heart that everything was going to work out, because God was looking out for me. When I arrived at my unt Mia's home, I gave her $100 for rent. I spent the first week searching for a new job. I was great at administrative work and I searched endlessly.

By the end of the first week, I applied for an administrative assistant position working for the Dean of Students at the George Washington University. The following week, I received a call to interview for the position. I was very excited and hopeful. My Unleashed Faith was working in my favor.

The morning of the interview, I thought positive thoughts. I thought about my clutching the Bible and the scripture. I said to myself, "I am more precious than the fowl of the air and God takes care of them."

I travelled to Washington, D.C., interviewed for the position with excitement. The Dean's executive introduced himself. His name was Dan. He had bright red hair, blue eyes, slender, about 5'10. He asked me the standard interview questions. Dan stated he was impressed with my work experience at the law firms and George Mason School of Law. Dan explained that if I were hired I would provide administrative support to the Dean of Students as well as the Director of Disability Support Services. I was excited about the position and I had the desire to work on a college campus again. Dan asked me to take a typing test in which I had to draft a professional letter. Dan was looking for professional content, proper greeting, grammar, and proper salutation. With excellence, I passed! After the test, Dan asked me if I had any additional questions and I stated, no. I followed up my visit with a sincere thank you for him taking the time to interview me.

The following day, I received a call that I was hired! Wow, what joy! The Unleashed Faith was, in fact, working in my favor! I got on my knees and thanked God for my blessing. I had a new job and a new beginning!

The New Chapter

I had such gratitude for the new beginning. On my first day of work, I got up early that morning and put on a professional black skirt, white blouse, black jacket, and high heels.

I arrived at 2121 I Street, NW The Dean of Students Office at The George Washington University with joy and excitement. A new journey and new beginning awaited me and I was eager to begin working. The George Washington University is a private university that is in the heart of Washington, D.C. The university resides near famous landmarks such as The Kennedy Center, The Washington Monument, and The White House. I was more than excited to roll up my sleeves and begin my journey working with the Dean of Students. My UNLEASHED faith was working in my favor.

When I arrived at the office, Dan greeted me with a huge smile and a hand shake. He said, "Welcome to the Dean of Students Office and Disability Support Services Office." He showed me around the office and introduced me to my new colleagues. He introduced me to, Kate, an administrative assistant. Carol, The director of Disability Support Services and Lori, The Dean of Students. After the formal introductions, I was escorted to my desk. My desk was in the front of the office. Part of my duties was to greet administrators, parents, and students.

During my lunch, I became familiar with the university campus. The George Washington University has an urban style busyness. The college has undergraduate and graduate programs, a medical school, and law school. The George Washington University also has a hospital associated with the college. The hospital's name is The George Washington University Hospital. It is rumored, many politicians have been patients at this hospital.

This new beginning energized me. I was eager to learn and work alongside my new colleagues. I found a new opportunity and I was going to use it toward my advantage.

Discovering Talents

Each morning, I would commute from Woodbridge to Washington DC. I would arrive at the commuter lot at 5:45 am to catch the 6:00 am commuter bus to Washington, DC. Then I would take the subway to the Foggy Bottom station. 2121 I Street was a short walking distance. The commute, one way, was two hours.

During my commute, I read books, thought about my goals, or talked to the person sitting next to me. Once I arrived at work, I was ready to dive into my duties. Dan would assign me tasks and I finished them in a timely manner. Dan worked as Lori's executive assistant. Lori had many responsibilities as the Dean of Students. As the Dean of Students she was responsible for the students. Lori was also responsible for planning programs for student life.

Lori was a tall, slender elegant woman. She was a southern woman from Louisiana that embodied southern sophistication. She wore her short black hair in an elegant bob. I was impressed with her style.

Lori's responsibilities were extensive. She would attend meetings with the president of the university and other administrators. Dan's responsibility was to manage Lori's schedule and to ensure the office ran smoothly.

Since I was quick to complete my assignments and I paid great attention to detail, Dan informed me that I would be given additional duties to assist the director of disabilities with projects. I gladly accepted these duties.

Carol was the most disorganized administrator that I had worked with. Her office was a mess!. Carol was disorganized and when you entered her office, there was no space on her desk. Carol's office reminded me of a disheveled professor. I was often assigned the task of organizing her office. When attending meetings, Carol often ran late. Lori and Carol were completely opposite.Lori's office was clean and precise and she was prompt for meetings. Lori always had the boss lady presence and at times it could be intimidating.

Even though Carol was disorganized; she was approachable. Carol had the warmest smile and she had compassion for others. Since I had been through recent trials, I immediately fell in love with Carol's compassion for others. I immediately compared Carol's compassion for others and Lori's accuracy, precision, directive style of management.

The Disability Support Office served to support students with accommodations as they were enrolled at the university. The Americans with Disability Act served as the cornerstone in which the accommodations must be adhered. I therefore was thrust in a new discovery. I began to learn how to accommodate people with disabilities to support them on their journey to receive their education. I learned how to support the blind student, the student with traumatic brain injury, the student with dyslexia, the student with cancer, the obese student, the student that was paraplegic. Carol's responsibilities were great and my new responsibilities were to assist her in any manner possible; I did it gladly.

Meeting Randy

It was exciting to assist many students achieve their educational goals. I assisted providing accommodations for students with disabilities. If a student were blind, I was responsible for hiring student readers, note takers and, proctors for exams. Each semester, I worked with approximately 200 students that needed accommodations. It felt great to be Christy's assistant. I felt as if I were making a difference.

One afternoon I was sitting at my desk, and a tall, handsome black man walked in the office. He walked straight toward my desk. As he approached my desk I greeted him with a warm welcome. I said; "Hello, may I help you?". When he responded his speaking voice was muffled. Kate, sitting at the desk behind me said, "Stacey, he is deaf. He cannot speak. She said it is going to be easier for you to talk if you write to each other." I said, "ok!" Immediately, I placed a piece of paper and pen on my desk. I looked him in the eyes and smiled as I handed him the pen and paper. Reluctantly, he took the pen and paper. He looked at me and poked out his lips. His eyes looked into mine! I was intimidated. He began to write. While he was writing, I waited patiently. He wrote; "Hi, my name is Randy." I wrote, "Hi, my name is Stacey" He wrote, "is Carol here?" I wrote, "No, I am sorry. She left for a meeting?" Again, he looked at me with an intense stare. He began to write again. The next sentence would allow me to discover a new gift placed in my life. He wrote, "if you are going to work here than you should learn sign language". I looked at him with a puzzled look. He began to write again. He said, "There are many deaf students on this campus. When we come into this office the only person that can speak sign language is Carol. If your going to work with her, than learn sign language!' I told him I would ask Carol about it when she returned. Randy wrote, "ok, also tell Carol to contact me when she returns." I wrote, "I will and have a good day." He smiled, looked me in the eyes. Again, I was intimidated. He stood and walked out of the office. I turned and gave Kate a bewildering gaze!

Kate returned my look and said, "Randy is an advocate for the deaf. He is an employee. He wants people to know how to communicate properly with deaf people when they come into the Disability Support office." I said; "I understand."

When Carol returned to the office, I told her Randy stopped by. She smiled, and said, "he can be a hoot!" I said; "yes, he told me if I should learn sign language." She said, "don't feel the pressure." I said, "how can I learn it?" She said, "I teach it on campus." I said, "really?" She said; "The winter semester has already begun, however, if you're serious about it, you can enroll in the summer." I said, "I am going to most definitely enroll."

Kate

Kate was the senior administrative assistant. She worked at the university for more than 10 years and her goal was to retire from the university. Kate was a native of Washington, D.C. She often spoke about her family and her upbringing. Kate had one daughter. Kate was a tall woman, dark complexion, she always wore her hair in braids, she had a gap in her two front teeth. Kate was reserved and had a pleasing demeanor.

After a few months, Kate and I became close. She often asked me about my family. One day she asked me about my religious beliefs. She asked me if I went to church. I informed her that I believed, but I did not attend any church.

Kate and I spoke often about my past and how I struggled with my relationship with my mother because of my leaving home and the lack of support. I also shared with her my disappointment in dating. One day Kate said, "Stacey would you mind if I prayed with you." I said, "right here in the office?" She said, "yes!" I was nervous about it, but I said "ok." We both stood and she placed her hand in mine. Kate prayed for my life and for me to seek God's guidance as I struggled with my past disappointments.

Kate's and my working relationship was becoming very close. I began to look up to her. She was like a big sister to me.

Sofia and Lawson

My work life was balanced and I was getting comfortable with the commute and work environment. I anticipated lots of opportunities while working at George Washington University. During the week, I spent most of the time commuting and working therefore there was little time for myself.

On the weekends I spent time at my Aunt Mia's home. Mia was married to Lance. Mia and Lance had two children, Alisha and Patrick. Mia and Lance were not a happy couple. They fought a lot. As a recreation, they dabbled in drugs. Their drugs of choice were marijuana and cocaine. I certainly did not approve of the lifestyle and on the weekends, I spent a lot of time thinking about my goals and aspirations. On Sunday mornings, I would frequent the Friendly's restaurant and review my goals and pray. I watched families enjoy their meals.

When I returned to my aunt's, I would help her make Sunday dinner. My aunt and I would talk about the family and how everyone was doing. My aunt told me that her brother-in-law, Tom, was going to move into the home until he could get back on his feet. She told me Tom would sleep in the basement. Now my aunt and Lance had another person to join them with their recreational habit.

One evening, I went to bed and Alisha decided to sleep in the room with me. During, the middle of the night, she left the room and slipped into her parents bedroom. When I awoke, Tom was standing in the doorway staring at me as if he wanted to approach me. I laid there for a quick second and then I abruptly jumped out of bed and shouted, "what do you want?".

Quickly he turned and left. I locked the bedroom door and thought to myself. I cannot let that happen to me again. I needed to move.

I told my aunt about the incident and she showed very little concern regarding the situation. I called my mother. My mother encouraged me to get in touch with my cousin, Sofia. Sofia lived in Dale City which was about 10 minutes from where I was staying. I called Sofia and she invited me to come stay with her and her husband, Lawson. I accepted her invitation and immediately moved in with her. Sofia and Lawson had one teenage son, Lawson, Jr.

My cousin and her husband welcomed me with open arms. They lived in a nice split foyer, I stayed in the "pink" guest room. When living with relatives, you get to witness the ins and outs of their personalities and lifestyles. My cousin's husband Lawson was a government employee. He was a fitness fanatic, he worked out most days of the week, he ate a very clean diet that consisted of little processed or boxed food. Lawson was a dedicated Pentecostal worshiper.

My cousin, Sofia, reminded me of my grandmother. Sofia was very spirited and she always said what was on her mind. Sofia often spoke of my grandmother and her love for her.

Sofia and Lawson attended church regularly and on several occasions I was asked to join them. One Sunday, I took them up on their offer and attended. The church was very lively with praise and worship. I enjoyed hearing the congregation sing songs of praise? Both the pastor and his wife were ministers. The sermon was very charismatic. After church, Lawson and I spoke about the church. He encouraged me to attend the following week.

When I returned to work, I was excited to tell Kate about my experience; she also encouraged me to attend services the following week. The following week, I attended church. I was eager to sing along with the praise and worship team. The pastor spoke another charismatic sermon. At the end of his sermon, he invited people to recommit their life to Christ. My heart began to beat faster, my breathing became shorter, I felt the desire to recommit my life, to start a new beginning with Christ. I said excuse me to the people sitting next to me as I scooted toward the aisle. Once I was in the aisle, I raised my hands in the air and walked toward the center of the stage. Once everyone was at the front of the church, we were instructed to bow our heads and repeat the sinners prayer and recommit our lives to Christ. I did so with an open heart and this re-dedication helped me focus tremendously on my spiritual growth.

After my re-dedication, I focused on work and studying the word of God, reading my bible, prayer and church.

On Solid Ground

For the next few months, I focused on work and my spiritual walk with God. Kate and I would often pray for each other. I enjoyed living with Sofia and Lawson, but at times their marriage reminded me of my grandparent's relationship, love and resentment was the core foundation.

I felt the desire to have my own space. I began to plan to move into an apartment of my own. I saved money for several months and within a few months, I moved into my own apartment. The freedom of independence in my own space, no words could compare. My feet were, finally, placed on solid ground.

My one bedroom apartment was very peaceful. I had everything I needed. After a long day at work and the 2 hour commute, I would enjoy a nice dinner, shower, read a scripture and retire for the evening. During the weekend, I would enjoy shopping, reading my bible, spending time with new friends that I met at church. On Sunday's, I went to church, enjoyed making Sunday dinners, and prepared for the upcoming week. The busyness of focusing on my new spiritual walk and settling into my new apartment kept me focused until it was time for me to register for the Sign language course schedule to begin in June.

A New Language

The winter semester was complete at GWU and I was anxious to begin learning American Sign Language. I enrolled in the summer course and for two evenings a week for two hours an evening, I immersed myself in studying, ASL(American Sign Language) and learning about the deaf culture.

First I learned how to finger spell and learn proper ASL Linguistic Syntax. ASL is a visual language and when speaking sign language it is very important to use facial expressions and emotions. I was smitten and intrigued about the deaf culture and the language spoken. Randy stopped by the office and offered his assistance with helping me study. I took him up on his offer and Randy and I began having lunch 1 hour a week for him to coach me. I began to progress quickly. Carol became impressed with my rapid progress. She encouraged me to continue studying the language. Unfortunately, ASL, was only taught as an elective and if I wanted to study ASL further, I would have to enroll at The Northern Virginia Community College, NOVA, in Alexandria, Virginia. That summer I spent concentrating on developing my sign language skills and planning for the fall semester at NOVA. During the Fall semester, I enrolled in a Saturday morning class to broaden my sign language skills. I participated in weekend Silent Suppers, which were arranged by deaf organizations. The purpose of the silent suppers was to allow a social activity where the deaf and hearing could communicate. The silent suppers allowed for me to practice ASL with people other than Randy and Carol.

The word spread on campus that Carol's assistant could speak ASL. Deaf students would stop by the office more frequently, I developed great relationships with the sign language interpreters hired to work with students. I felt part of the inner circle with the deaf students on campus.

Grief and Loss

Everything was finally settling down for me and I was relaxing in my apartment. I was infatuated with learning about the deaf culture and sign language.

I began to visit my mother, grandfather, and stepdad at least once a month. The vibrant side of myself was emerging. My mother would prepare family Sunday dinners. The family bond was becoming closer. I would travel back to Pennsylvania at least once a month to see my family.

During one of my visits my mother told me my grandfather was not feeling too well and he would be going to the doctors. The following week, my mother called me and told me my grandfather was admitted to the hospital. The following Saturday, I drove to Altoona, Pa where he was admitted. The family gathered to hear the doctor's diagnosis. The physician informed the family that my grandfather had an aggressive form of pancreatic cancer. Our hearts were crushed! One year prior, my grandmother died! The shock riveted the room. I remember running down the hospital hallway, tears streaming down my face. I tried to catch my breath. I just let the tears roll as I gazed out the window. I waited until my tears stopped before taking the long walk back to my grandfather's hospital room. He laid in the bed and looked at the family, he did not say much.

When he came home from the hospital my mother became his primary care taker. She moved my grandfather into her and my stepfather's home. My mother worked endlessly to make my grandfather comfortable. As his health declined, I witnessed the pain she was going through.

I would travel home most weekends to spend time with my grandfather and to provide my mom a much needed break. I would talk to my grandfather and ask him questions. I would try to make him laugh. It was like I was repeating the same experience that I had with my grandmother.

My grandfather was born in South Carolina. He grew up with his mom and siblings. His father died in prison. As a young adult, my grandfather transitioned to the north during the Great Migration. The Great Migration was a movement in which African-Americans moved from the rural south to The Northeast or West. He was hired to work in the brick yard. He remained employed there until he retired. During my Grandfather's illness, he became very quiet. I would often ask him what he was thinking and he expressed how disappointed he was that his illness came upon him one year after his retirement.I just listened and provided comfort.

When my grandfather was sleeping, I would spend time with my mother and stepfather. I began paying attention to my stepfather's need for constant oxygen. He consistently had a shortness of breath. My stepfather had sarcoidosis. Sarcoidosis is a lung disorder. One evening during dinner, I asked George if he believed in God and the savior Jesus Christ? He responded by saying; "no".

When I travelled home after that visit my heart was heavy. I was worried about George's health, he could not walk long distances. I prayed about his relationship with God the most. I prayed about how I could share the love of Christ with him without being overbearing. After pondering, I thought that I would make him instrumental gospel jazz tapes. George loved jazz! This is what I did, recorded gospel jazz cassettes for him. The following weekend, I was excited to give him his gift. When I gave it to him he smiled and then I told him it was gospel jazz music. He listened to the cassettes and he said he liked them. I was on a mission to share the gospel of Christ through music with George.

My grandfather's health was rapidly declining and it was taking a toll on the weekly care-givers. I felt such compassion for my grandfather there was nothing anyone could do. One of my grandfather's last request was to move back in his home. My mother and George made arrangements to move him back.

My sleep was uneasy during these times. I had vivid dreams about life, about death, about God, about people's souls, about spirituality. One night I had a dream that scared me. I dreamed that there was a casket, fallen snow, gray skies, and me hugging and comforting my mother. I awoke from the dream in such sorrow.

During my next visit with my grandfather, I laid next to him. I held his hands when he was in pain. I smiled at him, I made him laugh by wearing all his favorite hats. I asked him about life and he looked at me and said; "always work hard and it will pay off." He was weak, his 6 foot frame was skin and bones. The cancer was rapturing his body.

I returned to my apartment knowing these were my grandfather's last days. One evening, I had a dream, In the dream I heard my grandfather's voice, he said, "thank you for taking care of me and holding my hand." I awoke unsettled! The next morning, I received a call from my mother that my precious grandfather died. Relatives traveled to pay tribute to the patriarch. My grandmother died in September 1990 and my grandfather died in August of 1992. My grandmother always said my grandfather would proceed her in death shortly after hers. As weird and disturbing it was to hear her say it, their deaths were close together.

After my grandfather's burial, the following weekend, I went home and took George a gospel cassette. It was George's Birthday Month and my mother was planning a birthday party for him. I did not want to attend, I was wrapped in my grief. My mother said; "we are going to celebrate because life still goes on." That evening, friends and family celebrated George's birthday.

As the summer was winding down, I frequently went home to visit mom and George. My mother was busy with projects, reorganizing my grandfather's home. My mother decided to move into my grandparent's home. George and I would talk about his spiritual beliefs. I told him about the love of Christ and stated, I hope he accepts Christ into his heart. During one of my visits, my mother told me George accepted Christ into his life. I smiled and gave George the biggest hug. My mother also stated, George's complications with sarcoidosis were becoming more acute. His breathing was becoming more difficult. He had trouble walking long distances, he did not have the oxygen capacity in his lungs. During our dinners, I would sit and observe my mother and George. Their marriage was only three years young; however they began dating when I was 14 years old. I was happy when the got married. Their wedding was absolutely beautiful. My mother was radiant, her smile was bright and her eyes gleamed. The church was packed with family and friends to celebrate their union.

Thanksgiving was coming and I informed my mother that I needed to spend a few weekends in Virginia to catch up on rest. She understood and said she looked forward to my visiting at Thanksgiving.

Thanksgiving was here and I went home and helped my mother prepare dinner. It was an awkward Thanksgiving. At one time our Thanksgiving was full of family gathered at the table. This Thanksgiving was different it consisted of only my mother, George, and myself. We sat at the small round table in the dinning room. It was quite and dinner and the mood was awkward. I sat and observe my mother and George. I became disheartened, as I stared more intently at George, something told me He was next to die.

After Thanksgiving, I travelled home and embraced the serenity of my apartment. My routine was back to normal, commuting, working diligently at GWU, and practicing ASL with, Randy. My sleep was becoming regulated and I had more energy. At times, I would think about George. I would call home and speak to him and my mother. We would discuss the upcoming Christmas Holiday.

George would not live to enjoy Christmas. On December 9, of 1992, George was rushed to the hospital in the middle of the night. My mother called me crying hysterically, George's heart failed and his lungs did not have oxygen capacity to assist him with surviving. His organs began to fail and he went into a coma, never to awake.

My mother was in the forefront of planning the families third funeral within two years. The biggest blow my mother lost her father and husband within six months of each other. At times, I would look at my mother, She was trying to be strong, she tried to smile through the grief and pain. I would ask, "mom are you ok?" Her response was, "I am fine!" I knew she wasn't, how could she be fine?. God has a reason for everything and bad things happen to good people.

My sister could not travel from the Netherlands to attend the funeral. The day of the funeral family gathered to comfort my mother. Everyone gathered at the cemetery. It was cold that day, the sky was gray, and there was snow on the ground. My mother waited until everyone left the grave site. We both stood in silence and looked in sorrow, in shock and disbelief. I placed my arms around her and we slowly walked away, I kept hugging her and then I held her hand. I remembered the dream I had a few months prior, and was astonished of the accuracy.

These three deaths brought me to an awareness that life is precious and our loved ones should be cherished.

Seclusion

After the loss of my loved ones , I felt such grief. Emptiness filled my soul. I was longing for purpose in my life. I prayed about it day and night. I would talk to Kate about it and she prayed with me and suggested I begin to journal. I thought it would be good for me to write out my thoughts. For the next two years, I placed myself in seclusion. I would go to work and when I arrived at home, I would not watch television, I was single therefore I had no interruptions from anyone. When I arrived home, I would study ASL, pray and journal. I asked God continually "What was my purpose in life?" I began contemplating to return to college to earn the bachelors degree that I longed for. I was afraid I would fail. The other times I tried, I lacked the financial and family support. I was uneasy with the idea. I was settled at my job and I was content until the day Lori took me out to lunch.

One morning, when Lori arrived at the office, she said, "Stacey, I would like to take you out to lunch. Do you have lunch plans?" I nervously responded, "no!" I can go out to lunch today."She smiled and said, "Great, we will leave at noon." I nodded and smiled back and said; "ok."When she left, I quickly looked at Kate and asked her; "What was that all that about?" Kate shrugged her shoulders and said; "You're just going to have to go and find out."

At noon, Lori and I walked down I. Street toward Pennsylvania Avenue. The hustle and bustle of professionals and students briskly walking toward their desired destinations distracted me and took my mind off why Lori invited me to lunch. Lori and I decided on a place to eat. After ordering our food, Lori gazed in my eyes and asked how I was doing with the recent loss in my family and I told her I was doing ok. I asked her about her family and she always talked about her love and passion for Louisiana and how much she missed being there. I was un-settled and not relaxed during our conversation, something felt awkward.

We began to eat lunch and then Lori, placed her utensils down and said; "Stacey, there is something that I need to speak with you about." I said; "sure." She proceeded to say, "You have been working with me for three years now and you have done an excellent job and you have learned sign language, which is impressive." I said; "Thank You." The next words spoken by her echoed in my ear and when she spoke them I had to ask her to repeat the words twice. Lori said; "Stacey, it is time for you to move on. You have outgrown your position working with me." Silence and more silence. I asked; "Am I being fired?" She giggled and responded; "no, I just think it is time for you to move on." I was numb and did not respond. Lori said; "Stacey, please take your time finding a new job and please let me assist if you need it, I will give you a glowing recommendation." I thought; "Okay!" And then I thought; "Lori, you will be the last person on earth that I will utilize as a reference."

That weekend I went to church and prayed. After church, I went for a long walk. I remember looking toward the sky and asking God to guide me. I said to the heavens the scripture; "God, lead me and guide me in the direction in which I shalt go!" To this day, when I am confused about the direction of my life I repeat to myself, "God lead me and guide me in the direction in which I shall go!" Psalms 5:8.

Lori's lunch with me stirred my survival instincts. I felt like a lone wolf that had to find my calling, I had to make another pathway for myself.

Taking The Risk

Immediately, I began looking for a new job. Lori asked me if I needed to use her for a reference. I politely responded, "no."

After daily prayer, I decided to return to college. I applied to attend George Mason University. I was accepted to the University and was approved for student loans. The loans would assist me with college expenses and my rent. I decided to major in Individualized Studies. This Degree is geared toward adult learners. They have the ability to create their own major. I decided on Deaf Theatre Communications with a minor in Dance. I got a part-time job at the Disability Support Office at George Mason University.

A new opportunity was upon me, and I was excited to transition to GMU. I did very well, I was excited to be in the college environment. I was confident about my future. I threw myself into my studies, I was very content and I made the Dean's list. I enjoyed the arts and my enrolling in dance and acting classes energized me. The only sadness that remained in my heart was my struggle with the deaths of my grandmother, grandfather and Gene.

During orientation I remembered that there was a free counseling center for full-time students. I made an appointment and was scheduled to see doctor Dr. Kent. Dr. Kent was a very handsome light-skinned African-American man. He had class, style, and sophistication about him. Doctor Kent, asked me what brought me into see him and I told him I was grieving the loss of family members. He listened and took notes. Doctor Kent, kept noticing my eyes would gaze toward a brochure on depression. He said, "Stacey, are you depressed?" I shrugged my shoulders, and responded, "I don't know." Doctor Kent looked gently in my eyes and said, "please take this small quiz." I said, "ok!" I answered the questions honestly. I gave Doctor Kent the quiz and he reviewed the results. He looked at me and said softly, "Stacey, you may be suffering from severe depression." I did not say anything, I listened. He said, I would like to see you on a weekly basis. I said, ok. He encouraged me to continue to focus intently on the things that I enjoyed. I shook his hands and made the appointment for the following week.

Until our next session, I focused on everything I enjoyed. I enjoyed the hustle of the college campus, the jazz dance class I was taking, the acting class that I enrolled, and the geology class. The week flew by and it was time for my next appointment.

Dr. Kent greeted me with a smile and he asked how I was doing and I told him I was doing well. He said, "good." We walked to his office, and we sat down. After a few seconds, he grabbed his note pad. I said nothing. I just starred at him. He said, "Stacey, tell me about your child-hood." I said, ok" I told him about the relationships I saw growing up with my grandparents, my families recreational drug use, my date rape relationship and how that lead to my being beaten. After telling him all this information, he said "Stacey, I recommend two things." I said, "ok". He said, "please join the date rape support group." I said, "ok." He then looked at me and said, "I am going to recommend you see me weekly." I just starred at him and said, "ok". He said, "you have had very little support and we need to build you a support system as well as revis-it some of your childhood experiences in order for you to understand and move forward." I said, "ok". He asked, "If I was going to be ok, and I said, "yes". He gently smile and said, "ok." I made my weekly appoint-ments for the next three months. I enrolled in the date rape support group, and I continued to study and do well.

I enjoyed the theatre and dance classes the most and I kept focusing on them. One day, my dance professor stopped me after class. She said, "Stacey, you are talented." I said, "thank you." She said, "Have you con-sidered, trying out for the Washington Redskins Cheerleading squad?" My eyes lite up! I was flattered! She said, " you learn choreography quickly and you have the All-American look. She said, "I use to be a cheerleader and I know the director. If I wanted to proceed with trying out she stated she would give me a glowing recommendation." She told me I was going to have to work hard, but she thought I could do it. She told me how to enroll in the preparation classes and she encouraged me to attend. I smiled and gave her a hug and said "ok!"

Burgundy and Gold

After my conversation with my professor, I was beyond excited! Immediately, I researched the cost of the Redskinette Prep Course. After reading the guidelines and cost, I decided to register. I prayed to God and said if it were in His will than it would happen! I was anxious to share the news with my mother. She was visiting me the upcoming weekend and I thought this could be news to pick up our spirits. When she arrived that weekend, I showed her around my apartment and I could tell she was proud of me. I asked her how she was doing and she said, "I am fine." I thought to myself, my mother is so strong. That weekend visited family. As the weekend came to a close and she was preparing to head home, we stood in my small dining room and I said, "Mom, there is something I want to share with you and she said, "ok." I said; "My dance professor has encouraged me to become an NFL Cheerleader for the Washington Redskins." My mother listened intently. I told her, with excitement, about the prep course and how I enjoyed taking classes in dance and theatre. My mother continued to listen intently. After explaining, I said with pride, "I am going to go for It!" I waited for my mother's response. There was a pause; she looked me in the eyes and said; "Don't you think that is out of your league?" I responded sharply, "No it is not out of my league!" I dropped the subject, we finished our visit and I hugged my mother goodbye. When she left, I felt empty. I needed a confidence booster. I talked to Dr. Kent about it, he encouraged me to audition.

One week prior to the prep camp, I tracked down Dave's phone number and left him a message. To my surprise, he responded and said he was happy to hear from me. I told him about my opportunity and he said, "Stacey, I am impressed." I asked, him what I should do. He said, "Go For It!" I know it sounds crazy that I would contact someone, out of the blue that hurt me, but I knew Dave always wanted me to push past my past and succeed. In this regard he would always tell me the truth. I was more than excited that he said, "Go for it!" I asked him about his marriage. He informed me his marriage ended in divorce shortly after they got married. I thought to my myself, "what goes around, comes around." By the end of our conversation, I received an invitation to have dinner and I accepted.

The next weekend, we met for dinner. It was like two old friends catching up. We laughed, we drank, we ate. I told him about my enrolling in George Mason University. He said he was proud of me. By the end of the evening, he invited me to his apartment. Dave was on track with his goals. He was practicing law, he purchased a luxury condo in Northern Virginia, he purchased his dream car - a black corvette. He told me in order to he was working part-time as a bouncer at a sports club. I asked him why, he stated, "to offset expenses." We ended our reunion with a passionate kiss. I was excited about the possibility of dating Dave again. I wanted to prove to him that I could achieve great things too. I left our reunion more determined to cheer for the NFL.

The prep course lasted two weeks. It began in the middle of March and aligned with my college spring break. It was perfect timing. I read the guidelines very carefully, I wanted this opportunity. I purchased the shorts, tops, leggings and I purchased new make-up.

Day one of prep camp began at 7 pm. It lasted two hours. I remember walking into the gymnasium. The room was full of beautiful women. Many of them current cheerleaders, women that tried out the previous year and then the new hopefuls.

The current cheerleaders introduced themselves to the students. Immediately, thereafter we began learning dance routines. The dance routines began with 32 counts. The purpose of learning these routines was to see how quickly we learned the routine, our overall performance and our sex appeal. It was an exhausting two hours, but I was excited about the opportunity. During our breaks the ladies that were auditioning would huddle and talk about what we were experiencing. One young lady, Brianna, introduced herself to me and I was pleasant to her and I introduced myself. Brianna was very attractive. She had dark hair, olive skin and a beautiful smile. I noticed she could not keep up during the routines, but I encouraged her to keep trying. Her body frame was short and stalky. When I looked around at the current Cheerleaders, they all had a similar body type. All of them were slim built with a tiny waistline. During the first day of the prep course, we were instructed the first round of cuts were based solely on the appearance of the ladies auditioning. Did you have the looks, the figure, the American girl next door type of look. As harsh as it sounded, it was the reality.

I liked Brianna and assisted her with the routines as much as I could. After the third day of prep classes, Brianna asked me to go out to dinner with her and I agreed.

After the class, we went to a nearby Dennys. She asked me the general icebreaker questions, where I worked, how I became interested in cheering, what I was studying. I answered her questions and asked her the same. She asked if I had a boyfriend and I responded, no. Brianna, wasted no time to let me know she was dating an attorney and she was excited about where their relationship was going. I listened as she described him. She talked about how handsome he was and smart and sexy. I told her I use to work in the legal field and use to work at the George Mason School of Law. Brianna said with excitement, my boyfriend graduated from that law school. I said; "Really?" I asked, "What is your boyfriend's name?" She responded, "His nickname is DJ; his real name is Dave." I responded, "You're dating Dave Johnson?" With excitement, she said, "Yes! Yes! Do you know him?". I leaned back in my seat, looked her directly in the eyes and responded, by saying, "yes, I know him. We dated for 3 years and I just spent last Saturday night with him." Brianna was shocked, she said "no!" I said, yes!" I described his car, his apartment. She said, "let's go over to his house right now!" I responded, "ok". We left the restaurant. While driving, I chuckled to myself thinking Dave still hadn't changed.

We arrived at Dave's condo. Brianna wanted to go in first and speak to him. With a smirk on my face, I agreed.Brianna entered the condo, after a short period of time, she opened the door. I followed her to Dave's bedroom. When Dave saw me, he said "holy shit!". Brianna started crying. I, on the other hand, began laughing. I said; "Dave you should know better than this! You just broke her heart." They began to argue. I kept laughing, shook my head and walked out of the apartment. I went home. I had no time for this type of drama. I had an opportunity to focus on!

The second week of the prep course became more difficult! The cheerleaders began placing young ladies in groups. The groups would perform the routines and hopefuls were separated according to how well they performed the routines. I was quickly separated in a group which the current cheerleaders were paying close attention. I was shocked and nervous. The chatter amongst the ladies in our group was that we were being closely watched because ladies from our group may become Cheerleaders for the NFL.

Making The Cut

The second week of prep camp was over and it was time for the formal auditions. I arrived at the audition early. I had to provide the panel with a professional headshot and swimsuit. After all the hopefuls handed in their photos and the director thanked everyone for coming out. She explained the auditioning process. She also stated the first rounds of eliminations had been made. Over 300 photos were collected, only 100 hopeful's names would be called. The director began to read the names of those that made the first cut! Number 63's name was called, Stacey Chatman. Oh my goodness! It was time to prove myself and to others I could achieve this goal.

The week was grueling, the hopeful cheerleaders were also auditioning with the current cheerleaders. The returning cheerleaders had to secure their positions as well. It was a very competitive environment and there would be two more rounds of cuts. The next round of cuts would eliminate thirty more hopefuls. The intensity, the focused that was required, there was no room for error with my dancing technique and style. The second rounds of eliminations occurred. I was still in the running. One more elimination to get through. The day before finals, I was given my final critiques. I remember the evening before the final audition. I practiced the routines to perfection. Once I got finished, I laid on the floor of my apartment and closed my eyes. I visualized my cheering at RFK Stadium, I could sense that it could happen.

The next morning the remaining seventy hopefuls arrived at the final audition. The director gave a pep talk and thanked everyone for trying out. After the warmup, we were separated into small groups. Each group performed the routines and were interviewed. Auditions were complete. The director and the cheerleading captains stood alongside her as she announced the 1995-1996 Washington Redskin Cheerleaders. Number 63, Stacey Chatman's name was called. I jumped up and down with the other cheerleaders that made the cut! I was very proud of myself. I did it! I achieved the ultimate!

Redskinette

After making the final cut, the real work began. I had to balance working 30 hours a week, rehearsals, and studying. I also continued my weekly meetings with Dr. Kent.

Being a Redskins Cheerleader was worth the exhaustion. Getting to know the other talented ladies selected was exciting.

In order to have a night of fun, the cheerleaders arranged an ice-breaker event at a local night club called Champions. A few of us met on a Thursday evening around 9 pm. When we walked into Champions, all eyes were on us. Quickly the word got out that Redskin Cheerleaders were present. As we walked to our table, I heard a familiar voice call my name. I turned to look and it was Dave. When he approached our table, he congratulated me. I smiled, chuckled and said, "thank you." I asked him how Brianna was doing. He did not answer the question and he turned and walked away.

As the cheerleaders and I enjoyed dinner a man approached our table and asked me if I wanted to dance. I smiled and said, "yes." He led me to the dance floor and we danced. After the first song, we danced another. He introduced himself. His name was Seth. I smiled and told him my name. I noticed he had a southern accent. I asked him where he was from and he said,"Bedford, Virginia." I said, "I do not know where that is?" He said, "Southwestern Virginia. He told me it was a small town near Roanoke, Virginia. He asked for my phone number. I thought he seemed sincere.and we exchanged numbers.

The next day, Seth called me. We had a pleasant conversation and scheduled our first date the following week. During our date, he told me about his family. He was raised by a single mother. His mother had Seth when she was in her forties. Seth never knew his father. He only heard stories that his mother told him. Seth described his mother's pleasant personality. I listened intently. I had compassion for him. I certainly could relate to how he was raised. After our first date, I agreed to another one. After that date, we began dating exclusively and I focused on school and cheerleading.

The cheerleaders practiced two or three evenings per week. We would learn sideline routines and pre-game and half-time routines. Cheerleaders were also scheduled to conduct personal appearances in the community.

The summer of 1995 flew by quickly. September came and it was time to rock the field as a Redskinette. RFK stadium was packed to capacity. The Redskin's band, cheerleaders and football players entered the field and the crowd went wild. The hard work and practices paid off. The fans were amazing. I will always remember the smiles of the fans, the impromptu pictures taken with everyone, and the performances. It was an honor to attend Joe Gibb's Hall of Fame induction. Cheering for the Redskins will forever remain a highlight of my life's journey.

Marriage, Family and Divorce I

Seth and I continued dating and after two years we got married. We eloped and only a few close friends attended. I did not tell my mother or father. My reasons for not inviting my parents were simple. My mother met Seth and she did not like him very much and I did not invite my father because our relationship was strained.

Seth and I moved into an apartment in Centreville, Virginia. We focused on our new beginnings as husband and wife. Seth worked as a security specialist with a government contracting agency. I continued to work at George Mason University. Five months after we got married, we found out that I was pregnant.

My first trimester was a difficult one. The morning sickness was constant. I had to quit my part-time job and suspend my academic studies. The lack of finances placed a strain on our marriage. Seth and I argued constantly about how we were going to make it. One evening we argued for five hours. When we went to bed, I began spotting blood. Immediately, I was taken to the hospital. The doctor informed us the baby was doing well but we should avoid any and all stress. I spoke with Seth and told him I wanted to visit my mother for the weekend; he agreed.

When I arrived at my mother's home that weekend she asked me why I got married without inviting any family. I thought that was a fair question and I answered her by saying, "you don't like Seth so why should I be a fake and invite people that are not in support of the marriage?" My mother said sometimes we do not realize how our actions hurt others. I took note of what she said. As I spent time with my mother I realized there was something different about her. I simply could not place my finger on the difference.

On Sunday, my mother asked me how I felt about going back to Seth, she encouraged me to stay until I was a few more months into the pregnancy. I thought about all the stress Seth and I were having. I called Seth and explained to him how I felt stressed and nervous. I wanted to have a healthy baby. Seth told me I could stay with my mother but as long as I stayed with her he would not support me in any way! Financially he would not send any money. I was devastated and needed to make an important decision. Reluctant to stay with my mother I made the best decision for me and my unborn child. I told Seth I would be staying with my mother a few months. Seth finalized our conversation by standing firm in his decision to not assist me. I asked him to understand and hung up the phone. The following week, I made a doctor's appointment with my mother's obstetrician. Since Seth was not going to support me while I stayed with my mother I applied for government assistance "welfare". I thought to myself how does a person go from cheering on the sidelines for the Washington Redskins to applying for welfare. This is when, I knew my marriage to Seth may have been a mistake. I received assistance and I knew I was not going to remain a product of this dismal situation.

When my mother arrived home from work, I would inform her of my experiences of the day. My mother would listen and sometimes respond with ridiculous statements. She would tell me she was too young to be a grandmother. I would remind her she already had a granddaughter. It didn't make sense. One afternoon my mother was holding a small black bottle. I asked her if it was weed inside. Her response was this is much better than weed. I just observed because I was use to the recreational drug usage when I was growing up. When my mother took what was inside the little black bottle she became sweaty and anxious. For hours I would watch her walk through the house and not complete anything. She would wake up the next morning and go to work and do the same routine most evenings. I observed her and asked her again what was in the black bottle, she responded, crack! I did not know what that was, I was use to my mother's weed on occasion but nothing like what I was witnessing. I told family members about my mother's crack use. They brushed me off stating I was being a drama queen.

I spent most of my time in the bedroom in which my grandmother and grandfather died. I prayed for my life, my mother's life, my unborn child's life. My mother's habit was not getting better only worse. Her habit was beginning to effect her work and she was beginning to call out frequently. At least once a week Seth would call and check on me. I could not hide what I was going through. He became upset and stated the pregnancy was in the second almost third trimester therefore I should consider moving back to Virginia. Seth told me he and a friend had rented a multi-level townhouse and that we would have access to the top level. That evening, I got in my car and drove to my childhood pastors house and she and her husband listened intently about everything. The Pastor's wife worked at my mother's job and had heard rumors regarding my mother's addiction. I just listened. The pastor and his wife prayed with me and encouraged me to stay with them that night in their guest room. The next morning, I was greeted with a nice breakfast, compassionate hug and smile. We prayed one last time and I left to return to my mother's house.

When I arrived home the house was in disarray. Dishes remained in the sink, the dinner being prepared never got finished. I began cleaning the house and my mother came out of her bedroom still intoxicated from the night's activity before. Se called out sick. I didn't say anything except to tell her I was thinking about moving back to Virginia with Seth. She said she thought that was best for me and the baby. I called Seth and let him know I was ready to come home. Over the brief months I stayed with my mother we managed to buy items at yard sales for the baby, I spent that week organizing and planning.

The following weekend Seth arrived, we talked about everything and decided it was time for me to move back with him. My mother and Seth said very little to each other. I told my mom I was worried about her. She assured me she was going to be okay. Seth and I packed me and the baby's belongings and we arrived at the new townhouse in Virginia.

When we arrived home, I walked in our bedroom and noticed burnt candles. As we were unpacking Seth received a call from a woman. He tried to deny it was a woman's voice on the phone, but I kept pressing him to tell me the truth. Seth finally admitted he began seeing someone. He told me it was a new acquaintance. He thought our relationship was over and he thought he would move on. I thought to myself move on with me being seven months pregnant. My life was turned upside down. My only bright focus was giving birth to my child. The next two months, I spent arranging my doctors appointments and preparing for the arrival of the baby.

It was time for the birth of our child. The baby was overdue and I developed toxemia. The doctor scheduled to induce labor. I called my parents to let them know. That morning of the birth, I was excited and anticipated the delivery of our child.

We arrived at the hospital, Seth and I were escorted to the hospital room. The doctor arrived and informed me that I may have a long labor because I was only 2 centimeters dilated. I was induced and the journey of giving birth began. The doctor had to break my water, I still was not dilating. The doctor and nurses closely monitored my situation. All of a sudden, the baby's heart rate began to drop. The doctor announced that something may be wrong. I was immediately wheeled to the operating room for an emergency cesarean section.

When I awoke, Seth was holding our son, Jacob. Seth looked at me and gave Jacob to me to hold. When I got back to the hospital room, the doctor entered the room he looked at me with compassion. He took my hand and told me Jacob became detached inside of me. His heart rate decreased and Jacob and could have died. The doctor told me that I only had a five to six year possibility of having another child. I looked at Seth and thought about all the stressors. I just did not know if having another child would be possible.

Seth and I enjoyed the life that we had been gifted. Later that day my father, aunt, and cousin arrived. Seth's mother was planning to come spend a month with us to help us settle in with the new baby. My mother called me and stated she could not be there. I could tell she was not in a condition to drive down to be with us. I told her that by the end of the following week that it would be nice if she could come and visit her daughter and grandson.

After a few days in the hospital I was released. Seth and I got home and settled in with Jacob. Jacob became our main focus, he brought us back together to focus on the family. Seth got a part-time job and for the next eight weeks I focused on the transition as a new mother. I thought about how I was going to assist with supporting the family. I applied as a sales associate at the mall. I thought it would be good to work off hours so Seth could watch the baby and this would eliminate daycare expenses. Seth encouraged me to reach out to Carol to see if there were any jobs at George Washington University. I called Carol and she was excited to hear from me. She told me she was looking for an office manager to assist her with running her new office and student staff. I told her I would discuss this opportunity with Seth. Seth encouraged me to take the job at George Washington University and to place Jacob in daycare. I was reluctant to do so, but that was the best decision.

During the day Jacob attended a daycare near our home and Seth and I commuted an hour to work. Seth continued to work two jobs. I know that was difficult for him. After work, I focused on taking care of Jacob.

Going back to work at George Washington University was exciting. It was great to see familiar faces and get acquainted with new students and professionals working in the Disability Students Office. My duties were similar to the ones I had previously. The only difference was Carol's office relocated across the street. As I settled into my new position as office manager, being a new mom and wife, the commute, the daily life stressors, I noticed my weight from the pregnancy was not coming off. I was 75 lbs heavier than when I was cheering for the Redskins. My self-esteem plummeted.

To keep my mind pre-occupied, I focused on the upcoming holiday season with Seth and Jacob. My mother invited us to Thanksgiving dinner. Jacob was four months old and had not seen my mother since she visited him after he was born.

When we arrived to Pennsylvania for the Thanksgiving Holiday, I was in disbelief about what I was witnessing. My mother lost about 40 pounds, the house looked a wreck, there was no organization. I was taken aback and shocked.

I looked at Seth and he looked at me and he said things are getting bad for your mother. I just wanted to have a good Thanksgiving. The next morning I got up took care of Jacob, began cleaning the house and assisting with Thanksgiving dinner. I was disappointed, but I hid my emotions and thought about the good times that I had when the family gathered together during the Holidays.

After Thanksgiving dinner was prepared, my mother, Seth, and I and a few guests gathered in the living room. We joined hands to say grace. All of a sudden, my mother shouted I can't do this and left every-one standing in the living room. Immediately I went to check on her, she locked herself in the room and told me she would be okay. I slow-ly walked away from the door. I asked Seth what I should do and he shook his head and said her addiction is bad and if this is too much for me to handle we could cut our visit short. We left the next morning. I did not want Jacob, Seth, or me to deal with the toxic environment.

When we got home, I placed focus on Seth and Jacob. I thought about and prayed for my mother often. She would call on Sunday's in-toxicated and we could barely have a conversation, I listened. After we talked, I would shake my head and then immediately focus on Jacob and Seth.

Seth and I had a conservation about my returning to school on a part-time basis. As long as I worked at the university tuition costs would be covered. Due to our finances, I felt this was the best avenue for me to work toward completing my college degree. I planned to enroll in the winter semester. After the Holidays, I enrolled in college courses. I was excited about being back in college, however I knew I wanted to complete my degree at George Mason University where I had established most of my credits.

The next semester I auditioned for a play and got the lead part in the play American Dream. It was exciting to rehearse with students and complete the play. After completing the play, I spoke with Seth regarding my goals and specifically my finding a job at George Mason University. I also spoke about my desire for us to have our own apartment. Seth was in agreement with both. I was excited and began searching for a job and an apartment.

In January, I was hired to work at the Helen Kellar Institute of Disabilities as an administrative assistant. I was very excited and welcomed the opportunity. Once I could enroll in college and receive assistance, I did! I developed the road map that would allow me to complete my degree, work full-time and take college courses during my lunch or in the evening. Seth and I moved into our own apartment in Manassas, Virginia. In addition to my home, school, and worklife balance it was time for me to focus on my weight issues. I still was 75 lbs heavier than when I cheered for the NFL and it bothered me. I began to workout during free times and I enjoyed the discipline of a busy schedule. Life was busy but I could feel myself moving forward towards achievable goals. One year after working at George Mason University, Seth and I purchased a townhouse is Winchester, Virginia. The townhouse was affordable which was great. The commute was 1.5 hours. I got up at 4:30 am to go to the gym, I would make sure I was home by 6 am so Seth could leave for work. I would get Jacob ready for daycare and then leave immediately from there to go to work.

One day while sitting at my desk, I received a call stating that my mother was in trouble and I needed to go see her immediately. I arranged to take the next day off and drive to Pennsylvania. When I arrived at my mother's home, she laid on the floor looking hopeless and helpless. The addiction was overtaking her life. She had gotten involved with the wrong crowd and the drug use lead her down a road of destruction. My grandparents home looked like an addict's house. My mother's best friend came to see her. We both just stared and tried to ask my mother questions. My mother explained the packed boxes were to be taken to Georgia where she planned to live with my Aunt Mia. I told my mother that moving to Georgia was not in her best interest because my aunt was an addict. My mother stated she applied for partial retirement and would work part-time in Georgia. I looked at my mother's best friend and said this is too much. My mother's friend gave her a hug and left. I stood looking at my mother with bewilderment. I knew my mother was headed down a dark road. I refer to this time in her life as living her life in a dark cloud. I asked my mother if she had food, She stared at me. I told her I would go to the grocery store and purchase microwaveable dinners. After getting back from the store I asked her to reconsider her decision to move. I hugged her and left. I sat in my car tears streaming down my face, I cried so hard I could not see anything. All of a sudden, I heard a knock at my window. I wiped the tears from my eyes. My mother kept knocking on the window until I turned my head to look at her. When I looked in her eyes, I could see her sorrow and despair. I said mom I have done all in my power that I can do, the only thing I can do is pray for you to recover. I cannot go down this dark road with you. I left and drove to my grandparent's and stepfather's graves and prayed for her.

My mother moved to Atlanta with my aunt. She called to let me know she was okay. I said that I was glad to hear from her. I told my mother that I felt it best that we have limited contact because it was too much and I had enough to focus on with being a new mom, wife, school, work, and my own self-esteem issues. I needed space from my mother.

The Wrath Of Crack

When mother moved with my Aunt Mia I never felt at ease. My mother rarely lived outside the two stoplight town of Mt. Union, Pennsylvania. My mother was a hard worker and I admired her as a kid growing up. My resentment towards her began when she sent me away to the government program. I blamed her for my being date-raped. Now, the crack addiction was too much for me to grasp or accept. I had to remind myself I was a woman witnessing my parent struggle and suffer with addiction. I had my own child to nurture and this was not the life I wanted him to learn about or be around.

Co-dependency can be a struggle. Children and young adults wrap themselves up in the continual cycle of the feelings and emotions of the addict and they rarely ultimately take care of protecting themselves. I found myself being a co-dependent and being consumed by its harmful cycle. One of the wraths of addiction is that everyone hurts, the addict and the family members.

While my mother was staying with my aunt she would call and speak about her life in Atlanta. At first things seemed to be going well. As time went on things began to unravel for my mother in Atlanta. My aunt's life of addiction was showing signs of the wrath of crack. She lost her job, her home, and law enforcement was watching her. The wrath of crack was destroying her life. I felt compassion but what could I do? I prayed for my mother and aunt in Atlanta.

I continued to focus raising Jacob and focused on family, working full-time and taking college courses, and trying to lose weight. Any time my mother would call, I would speak to her. During one of our conversations, she stated she was living in a hotel and she was walking to work. I asked her about her health and her medications. She had not been taking them. My mother could not go without her medication. I became quiet and let her talk. She finished her conversation by asking if she could come live with me. I asked her to call my sister and ask her. A few days later, I received a call from my mother asking me again if she could come live with me. I became quiet and told her I would get back to her the next day.

When we ended our conversation, I became furious about the wrath of crack and its destructive cycle. Crack ruins people's lives. People lose their homes. They lose the respect of family and friends. Resentment toward my mother grew. I cried, I prayed to God to help me make this important decision. I did not want my mother dying in the streets of Atlanta. It had been four years since I saw my mother. I went home and explained all of this to Seth. He shook his head and said, "Stacey over the years this has added stress to your life. You do not owe anyone anything and you have enough on your plate. Can you handle this? Where will she sleep? The final decision will be yours. After Seth and I talked, I cried and prayed. All of a sudden I became quiet and placed the Bible in my hands and began reading a scripture. I read the scripture "Honor Thy Mother and Father." After reading the scripture, my decision was made and I let Seth know. We began planning to have my mother come live with us.

I called my mother and provided her three rules that she must adhere no drugs, get a job, and focus on getting her health together. My mother bought a bus ticket to arrive the following Saturday. Seth, Jacob, and I drove to pick her up at the bus station. When Seth and I saw her, she was so skinny and frail. It was like looking at a living ghost. My mother had not seen Jacob for four years she was amazed at how he was growing up. We drove away from the bus station and transitioned her into our home. After two weeks, she began looking for a job. Within a month she got a job at Sheetz, a franchised convenience store. Whenever she needed a ride to work, we provided it or she took a cab. My mother was slowly pulling herself back together.

Family, Marriage, Divorce II

As my mother's life was coming together, My marriage to Seth was being unraveled. Seth and I had many differences, a year prior to my graduation. I reminded Seth of the commitment we made that when I graduated from George Mason University that we would move to California.

One Saturday morning, Seth approached me. I was folding clothes and preparing to study. Seth looked at me with his big blue eyes and told me that he was not moving to California. He said that if I wanted to go for the purpose of my dreams then that was ok, but that Jacob would remain with him. I stood there exhausted and I reminded Seth that I was in my eighth year of trying to complete the degree. I revisited all the struggles that it took me to get to this point. I was less than a year from graduating. I stood there waiting for his response, he looked at me and said, "Stacey, your visions are not my visions and I am not moving from Winchester." My heart crumbled, I was hurt and angry. I worked so hard to create a degree that incorporated all of my passions. I looked at Seth with intensity and said to him; "how many dreams do I have to give up to be with you?" I said we have one more year before Jacob goes to kindergarten. I told him I wanted to be there in the morning when Jacob left for school and when he returned. Seth and I were not on course with this goal either. All the frustration caused Seth and I to argue constantly which was not good for my son, myself, Seth, or my mother. I firmly believe that people should not be a stumbling block to anyone's dream. Sometimes a dream, goal, or vision is all that someone has to hold onto. I created a motto during this time that began with "Do Not Let Others Control Your Destiny."

The year passed and I was working diligently to complete my degree. I had one more course to complete before earning my degree. I asked Seth about the move to California and he told me that we were not moving. It took me nine years to complete the degree. I felt like a success and failure at the same time. I was disappointed because I worked so hard at earning my degree but I was placed in the position of making the choice of either packing my bags and leaving to follow my dreams or make the best out of my situation.

I looked Seth firmly in the eyes and said to him with firmness, "My dreams you should not mess with." There were times in my life my dreams were all I had, they protected me from making destructive choices in my life. Working toward my dreams and aspirations made me happy. Firmly, I told Seth I did not think our marriage would last. With boldness I told him that I did not want him at my graduation. I also let him know the only people that I would invite would be Jacob and my mother. I also let him know that we needed to separate. He said that I would have to move out of the house because he was not moving. I was furious with him. I let him know that I would begin searching for an apartment. I also let him know Jacob was coming to live with me. Seth was angry and furious. I know I hurt him. Seth was a good dad and loved Jacob. I also let Seth know that I felt the degree I earned would become useless and that I could not consciously move across the country and not allow for Jacob to have the chance to remain close to his father. That day I made the decision to give up my dream of becoming an actor and living in California. On that day I also made myself the promise that no one would never stop me from achieving any other goal or dream that I was willing to work toward.

The day of graduation arrived and I was ecstatic! Nine years of struggles to earn the bachelors degree was finally over. My mother and son watched me walk across the stage and receive my diploma. I was very proud of myself and my accomplishment. I still have the picture on my night stand. When I glance at the picture I have the most radiant smile and I exude confidence.

After the graduation celebration I returned home and began planning the separation from Seth. I searched for an apartment and I was able to place a security deposit on a condo less than two miles from where we were currently living. My mother said she would assist me with expenses. I was watching my mother's progress. She was drug free and working. Once again, I unleashed my faith and decided to move. I was walking toward the unknown with my mother and son walking next to me. I was scared, however, I could not let fear overcome my decision to move forward in life. If I would have stayed with Seth, I knew I would become resentful and bitter towards him and I did not want to remain in a marriage that would cause me to despise him and not love him. I witnessed this kind of marriage with my grandparents.

When I moved, I felt independent to make choices to continue to move forward in my life. I began searching for a new job. In the meantime, I continued to work on losing weight, I worked out most days of the week and began taking kickboxing classes. The fitness instructor encouraged me to to become a fitness instructor. I was curious how to become an instructor, I asked him several questions regarding the process to become a fitness instructor. He suggested I speak with the group exercise coordinator regarding the procedures of becoming a fitness instructor. She told me about a kickboxing instructor training that would be in the area. She told me that if I attended the certification and became a kickboxing instructor that she would hire me as a substitute kickboxing instructor. I was very excited! Immediately, I researched the company providing the instructor training and enrolled. The day of the instructor certification I could hardly contain the excitement. When the conference presenter entered the room, it felt like magic entered the room. The conference presenter's name was Lacy. Lacy had an energetic and urban vibe. Lacy was fit, trim, and beautiful. She informed us the kickboxing company originated from California. Lacy informed us this was a different type of kickboxing class that had high energy music and had a supercharged fast drill in the middle of the workout and this unique drill is what would make our fitness members fall in love with the class format. The training lasted eight hours, by the end of the training I was enthralled by the program and for the first time connected to something since giving up my hopes of moving to California. When I got home, I shared my new passion for the program with my mother. I focused on learning the choreography and auditioning the format to the group exercise coordinator at the gym. After I auditioned the format, I permanently was scheduled to teach a Saturday morning kickboxing class.

I was on a new mission to learn as much as possible about the fitness industry. I was intrigued about the profession. While teaching part-time, I focused on finding a new job in which I could be content. I applied for a job as a behavioral specialist with a local human service agency. A behavioral specialist works with students with disabilities in the public school setting. The major role of a behavioral specialist is to keep the student on task. If the student should become off task due to emotional outburst or any other behavioral issues, the specialist provides therapeutic interventions. My experience working with persons with disabilities at the collegiate level and my work with deaf and persons with autism made me qualified for the position. I interviewed and was offered the position. This was a new career path because I also worked with emotionally disturbed children. Many of the emotionally disturbed children were being raised in dysfunctional homes. Sometimes these children would come to school ready to learn and sometimes their focus was off. As a behavioral specialist, it was my job to find out what the trigger was, provide therapeutic intervention, and keep the student academically on task. I worked as a behavioral specialist for two years. Unfortunately, in the second year, after working with a child for a few weeks, I was told because of my race, I could not work with the child. I found myself in the middle of a discrimination case. The agency in which I was working was found to be practicing discriminatory practices. For legal purposes, the intimate details of this case cannot be discussed. I was unemployed and after six-months of searching for employment, I was hired part-time to work as an executive assistant at the medical center. I also continued working part-time in the fitness industry.

I made the decision to place all my concentration on transitioning to working full-time in the fitness industry. The kickboxing company that I became certified to teach kickboxing was conducting auditions for promotional directors. If chosen, the promotional director would arrange instructor trainings and train instructors. Immediately, I contacted the president of the company and I was delighted to hear a response. I applied for the position and provided an audition tape. In a few weeks, I heard back from the company. I was selected to attend the audition in Southern California. I was finally going to California. My dreams of acting did not transpire, but my passion for fitness and wellness was becoming more apparent.

I was not going to travel to California by myself, a few months after Seth and I separated I began dating Kurtis. Kurtis wanted to support me as much as possible. He suggested that Jacob, and his son go to California with me. I was excited to be able to bring, Jacob and Kurtis and Kurtis's son. Kurtis and I met from a mutual friend. Kurtis grew up a few miles from my hometown. When it came to our core values we had a lot in common. We both grew up in the country and we both had a childhood that was dysfunctional. Kurtis's mother died when he was ten years old. His father raised him and Kurtis often spoke about his childhood disappointments and struggles. Kurtis moved to Virginia when he was 20 years old and began working at a construction company.

When Kurtis and I began dating he was divorced from his wife. Kurtis came into my life at a major transition and he provided the emotional support I needed. Kurtis got along great with Jacob. He took Jacob fishing and hunting. If there was anything that my son, mother, or I needed Kurtis ensured we had it. When I informed Kurtis that I had a chance to travel to California, he ensured me that everything would workout and I felt secure.

When we arrived in Southern California, it was amazing. I was embarking on a new opportunity. Kurtis arranged to spend time with the boys while I was training. I was grateful that I found someone that supported my dreams and embraced building a relationship with Jacob.

After everyone was settled, Kurtis drove me where the training was being held. He kissed me good~bye and wished me luck. I gave him a huge hug, looked him in the eyes deeply and said thank you.

When entering the hotel, I was escorted to the conference room where the training was being held. I received my name tag and audition materials. Each attendee was greeted by staff and we were instructed to mingle with the others until the training began. There was something about the audition that brought back memories of me auditioning for the NFL. The ladies were beautiful, fit, and multitalented. Many were married, running fitness businesses or professional women.

It was time for the training to begin and we all were eager to learn from the creator of the program. After the formal introductions, the creator entered the room. The owner of the program was absolutely stunning. She had black-hair, green eyes, 5"9", with a medium built.

She captivated the room with her vivacious energy and she was searching for the same type of people to represent her brand. The training consisted of three days of grueling workouts, presentations, and sales training. There were also individual interviews with the owner and her elite representatives. After the three days of training, I left feeling confident that I would be selected. I was eager to further my career in the fitness industry and I thought this would be an excellent opportunity.

All people that attended the audition were told they would be contacted in two or three weeks. I heard back from the director that I was selected to represent the State of Virginia as a promotional director.

During my eight years as a promotional director, I trained hundreds of fitness instructors in cardio-kickboxing, pilates & yoga, and dance. During this time, the owner and my mentor, became a celebrity trainer and multi-millionaire. I appeared in a fitness infomercial to represent my weight loss success. I travelled to California multiple times to train and motivate others to achieve their wellness and fitness goals. Even though it seemed like my fitness career with this company was the ultimate destination. I began thinking about how my success was entwined with my mentor's success. I decided to terminate my relationship with the company.

I began to make plans to begin my own company. After a few months of planning, I took $200 and started Xtreme Fit Studio. Beginning my own company allowed me the opportunity to provide fitness and wellness to people in my community. I also got to train fitness professionals. One of the first instructors that I trained remains as one of Xtreme Fit Studio's instructors. Beginning the company took a lot of hard work and perseverance. Lots of early mornings and late nights. Xtreme Fit Studio began making its mark in the community. The struggle of working part-time at the hospital and the daily operations of Xtreme Fit was a struggle.

Kurtis witnessed my dedication to running my company. Three years had passed since our first date. One evening, Kurtis surprised me and asked me to marry him and I said, "yes!" It was important to both of us to have a church wedding with family and friends. Kurtis was married two times and neither one of his previous weddings were held in a church. I remembered how, I eloped when I married Seth. It was important to me that we have a church ceremony to celebrate our love for each other.

The day of our November wedding was perfect! Family and friends attended. Both of my parents were present. I felt beautiful and Kurtis was my hero! I loved Kurtis's for many reasons, he loved my son, my mother and I unconditionally. He had a big heart, was a hard worker and an excellent provider. After our wedding, we took a cruise for our honeymoon.

When Kurtis and I arrived home, I asked Kurtis if I could dedicate 100 percent of my time operating Xtreme Fit Studio. Kurtis said, "Yes."! I was an entrepreneur! I was living in my purpose. God replaced one dream and provided me a new one. I worked diligently to fill my schedule with additional teaching classes. I was teaching eighteen classes a week and I became a wellness coordinator for a local government agency. For the first time, in a long time, I felt complete. Kurtis and I bought a spacious 4-bedroom home with a complete basement, which we converted into a home gym.

Life could not get any better, I was losing weight and feeling great. I felt my life was hectic, but I felt balanced. My mother was working full-time and she thanked me for assisting her with getting back on track with her life. I remember looking her in the eyes and saying I have been waiting to hear those words for ten years.

Troubled Waters

Kurtis began spending some time with Seth and Jacob to have male bonding. Periodically, they would go fishing or to the movies. When Kurtis got home I asked how everything went. After one of his visits with Seth and Jacob, Kurtis told me that Seth wanted Jacob to come live with him. I was hurt and confused regarding Seth's statement. Kurtis and I were focused on making my son happy. Jacob had everything a child could ask for. At times Jacob would become distant and I contributed it to the fact that he was a teenager. When this topic came up, I just told Kurtis we should make the house a happy household.

My mother and Kurtis had some health issues. My mother had successive health crises in a short period of time. At times, she was reluctant to seek treatment. Once my mother sought treatment for her medical conditions, she got better. Kurtis had a heart attack and he would have to take it easy and recover. Things were becoming very stressful at home and once again, I placed my energies on operating the business. Focusing on the success of the business was an escape for me. All other areas of my life, I felt like I became a caretaker to everyone. I felt a lot of pressure and at times, I became resentful. I just wanted people to take care of themselves. I encouraged them to eat properly and exercise. When I would encourage my mother and Kurtis to change their lifestyle habits, I was met with resistance. It was like I was speaking a foreign language. I wanted to give up, but I just kept going and tried to find ways to remain positive.

It seemed as if Kurtis and I were not connecting, we would argue a lot. He felt that I was focusing too much on the business and I was. I wanted the business to be successful. At times, I felt Kurtis was envious of my losing weight and becoming a more confident woman. At times,

Kurtis simply did not know how to speak to me. I was very defensive and our relationship was one of conflict instead of love and nurturing. Kurtis and I began discussing how unhappy our relationship was becoming. We both could be stubborn and neither one of us was listening to the needs of each other. The Holiday season was near and we decided to focus on Thanksgiving and Christmas.

We planned an intimate Thanksgiving dinner. My mother, Jacob and Kurtis would be the only ones attending. I always loved preparing Thanksgiving dinner and mastering the recipes. My mother and I split the responsibility of prepping the dinner. We spent most of the morning and early afternoon preparing, turkey, green bean casserole, macaroni and cheese and desserts such as pineapple upside down cake, jello, pumpkin pie and sweet potato pie. We decided to eat around four in the afternoon . I called Seth to let him know what time to bring Jacob home, Seth agreed.

Thanksgiving dinner was complete and the table was set, Four o'clock came and Seth was more than an hour late with bringing Jacob home. Kurtis was becoming angry. I called Seth and he apologized for his tardiness.

At 5:30 pm we managed to sit down and gather as a family. Kurtis still remained upset about us eating late. I told him to forget about it and focus on enjoying dinner. Kurtis stood up and began carving the Turkey. As he held the knife in his hand and began slicing, he turned and looked me in the eyes. He continued to stare at me and said with coldness in his voice, "This marriage ain't worth shit." I was silent. I felt like my bones in my body were shattering. I remained silent. I looked at Jacob and he bowed his head and slid down in his seat. My mother was silent. I said nothing and tears rolled down my eyes. When Kurtis witnessed the tears, he abruptly left the dinner table. I sat with my mother and Jacob and watched them eat. I did not have the appetite. I did not eat.

That evening, I began to question my happiness with Kurtis and our marriage. I felt like I needed to speak to a counselor regarding our relationship. Immediately following the Holiday, I spent time with a counselor. The counselor and I discussed the stressors that I was under on a daily basis. Regarding the marriage, the counselor and I discussed if I was truly happy. I was at another crossroads in my life. After a year of counseling, Kurtis and I decided to divorce. I broke the news to Jacob stating that I wanted him to see me happy. My mother thought Kurtis and I should try a little more. I told my Mother that she should begin making alternate plans. My mother told me that she planned to fully retire and move across the country with my sister. Kurtis moved into the guest bedroom and he told me that we had about ten months before everything would be final with the divorce. He suggested I make arrangements for me and Jacob.

I told Seth about the divorce. Seth suggested Jacob stay with him for a week. I thought it would be a good idea. I checked in with Seth and Jacob to see how everything was going. Seth wanted to arrange a meeting with me to discuss Jacob. I arranged for the meeting at my house. Seth, Jacob, and I sat at the kitchen table. I looked at both of them, there was an awkward silence. Jacob shyly, looked into my eyes. Seth began to speak slowly, he glanced in my eyes and said that he wanted Jacob to come live with him. I stood in silence before I said anything. I held back tears and asked Jacob if this is what he wanted. Jacob looked at me and said, Mom, I just want to try it. I softly responded to Jacob and said your Dad is not going to let you just try it. For me, I certainly remember what it was like not having my father around when I was growing up. Jacob asked if he could stay with Seth another week. I agreed.

Throughout the week, Seth called me and pleaded his case for reasons Jacob should live with him. He presented my upcoming divorce, my job, and the transition I was about to go through and last but not least this was something that Jacob wanted. Once again, the thoughts of me growing up with my father not being present flooded my memory. the emptiness I felt when there were no phone calls, hugs to greet me in the morning or gentle kisses to tuck me in bed at night. I could not deny my son living with his father. I let Seth know my decision.

The day that Jacob moved was difficult for me, I cried for hours. I laid in bed and held my heart, and then I wiped the tears from my eyes, washed my face and got in my car to teach my dance class. I felt like my maternal bond with my son was severed. Above everything, I enjoyed packing my son's lunch, putting him on the bus, picking him up from school, scheduling his appointments, helping him with his homework. In an instant, everything changed.

When I got home, I let Kurtis know about Jacob and he sat silently. He asked me if there was anything he could do. I suggested that we stop the divorce and try to work everything out. He sat with his back toward me and said, it was too late and that he already made plans to move forward and sell the house. I felt my life slipping away from me and there was nothing I could do to salvage it. I had to ride this storm out and have faith that everything would work out. The next day there was a For Sale Sign placed in the front yard.

Seclusion II

Everyone's lives were shifting, my mother moved to the Midwest to live with my sister. The day my mother left, I watched her get in the car and tears streamed down my face. My heart ached, I just let the tears stream. I sat on the steps for a while and did not think too much. After an hour, I stood up and walked into the kitchen and placed my keys on the counter. I locked the door behind me and left. I was headed to a room I rented from a colleague.

This transition was difficult for me, I was depressed and cried a lot. I felt the loss of family. In order to cope with the changes, I created new goals, I began training to compete in bodybuilding competitions, I produced a fitness video. I was offered a full-time fitness management position in Baltimore, Maryland.

After a year of living with my colleague, I found a tiny one-bedroom apartment. This apartment was my solitude from the world. I decorated it nicely. It reminded of a tiny New York flat.

I spent a lot of time in my apartment thinking about my life's direction. During this time, I evaluated who my true friends were. I became distrustful of people. I spent a lot of time alone. I consumed myself with work, working out, and planning my next competition. Jacob would visit me every other weekend. I promised him that I would not move until he graduated high school.

During this time, I tried dating, my being middle-aged and trying to learn the tricks of the game was not for me. There were some Dark Knights out there pretending to be everything that I needed. I quickly learned the rules of dating changed. Men and women communicate way too much through text messages instead of picking up the phone and talking. I was dating men that did not value a woman that holds herself to high-standards. I became disinterested in the dating game.

Sometimes on the weekend, after having a few glasses of wine, I would call my mother and speak to her about everything I was going through. I would tell her how I felt so alone, how I was in emotional pain and turmoil. My mother listened and told me that everything would work out. That is what I kept telling myself, I would repeat it to myself daily, that everything was going to work out and that my life would get back on track. In order to deal with the loneliness, I began going to church. I enjoyed the charismatic sermons. Attending church reminded me of the first church I attended.

The church offered workshops and I registered for the "Being Single" workshop. This workshop discussed the pros of being single. I remember walking into the first class. There were a few attendees gathered around Pastor Brett. Pastor Brett was 6'1", he had bright red hair, slim built, he wore glasses, and had the most generous smile. He welcomed me with a bold welcome and offered me a seat. I sat down and glanced around the room and looked at the other attendees. They had the same look I had on my face, perplexed! Pastor Brett began speaking about the objectives of the workshop which were to study people from the Bible that were single: Mary, Martha, Paul, Anna, Jeremiah, and John the Baptist.

Even though studying these biblical characters were helping me deal with being single, it was Pastor Brett's own story that intrigued me the most. Pastor Brett shared with us that he lost his parents and wife within a year of each other and in order to cope with the pain and loss he turned to drugs and alcohol. He spoke about how he lost everything. Pastor Brett lost his respected position as a Pastor of a mega church, family and friends alienated him. He disclosed that his turning point was when he was arrested and spent time in jail. Pastor Brett was rebuilding his life. After he shared his life experience, I sat and thought about my mother's pain and loss. For the first time, I overlooked her being an addict and I felt compassion for her pain. I understood her pain, her lack of support, and how she may have felt isolated living in a small town. Pain and isolation is a terrible thing to endure and without the correct support system, people may become prey to depression, despondency, and drug and alcohol addiction.

After leaving the workshop, I called my mother and told her I understood some of the reasons why she became addicted to crack. I no longer carried the resentment toward her. Pastor Brett became part of my support system. I continued to train for the competitions and focused on my duties in Baltimore. There were days where I struggled with feeling comfortable with where I was in life. This time in my life, I just kept telling myself that my life would become better. I listened to motivational speakers, I attended church, and kept working out, I achieved my weight loss goals of 114 pounds.I knew that my life would get better if I just remained hopeful.

Reconcilation

When Kurtis and I divorced, we both knew there were a lot of unfinished conversations that needed to be finished. The first year in my apartment, I made Thanksgiving dinner and invited, Kurtis and Jacob. We had a pleasant dinner. We gathered around the table and talked about Jacob's school, his band, and friends. Kurtis spoke about his job. I asked him if he was dating anyone and he said, no. I told Kurtis that I needed to practice forgiveness in order to move forward. I told him I forgave him. He looked at me and said he forgave me too. After Jacob left, Kurtis stayed and said he wanted to ask me a question. He went to his car and got a folder. Kurtis handed me the folder and I opened it. There were pictures of five houses. I asked Kurtis, why he was showing me pictures of houses. Kurtis glanced at me and said, He was getting ready to buy a home in West Virginia. He asked me to pick out the new home and move in with him. I took a few moments to think. I then looked at him with anger in my eyes, I said; "Kurtis, I have lost so much in this divorce how can I just turn back." There were times I felt like I was losing my sanity. Eventough I loved my apartment, I lost my home. I just could not take the risk again. I forgave Kurtis but I could not forget.

A year later, while driving home from work, I was in an automobile accident.The accident was minor, no injuries, but my car was totaled. The first person, I called was Kurtis. Coincidentally, he was less than a mile away. Kurtis showed up at the scene of the accident, he took care of all the details with the other drivers. He knew I was shaken up, he drove me home. The following week, Kurtis went with me to shop for a new car. From beginning to end, he was there to ensure, I was okay. During this experience, I knew that Kurtis and I may get back together. Just like when we met, he was there for me during my time of absolute need. I felt safe with Kurtis. I began to realize, he was the only man that I would fully trust. Kurtis is a man of his word and his action supports his words. For someone like me that grew up not trusting any man, except my grandfather, this was a breakthrough for me. I began to value Kurtis in ways that I did not when we were married.

After that moment, I continued to try to move forward with dating, but no relationship progressed to a level that Kurtis and I shared. I felt like a person only existing to make my dreams happen, but with no one to intimately share my experiences . I called my mother and she listened to me. My mother spoke to me gently and said; "Stacey, I think it is time to try to reconcile with Kurtis. She said, He still loves you. After I finished the conversation with my mother, I called Kurtis and I asked him if I could move with him to West Virginia. I was tired of being alone.

Kurtis came to my apartment that night and we talked and began making plans to reconcile. Even during this time of planning I was not fully sure that I should reconcile. In order to find resolution, I contacted Pastor Brett and told him about my situation, he said, "Stacey, God is a God of reconciliation." I sat and I prayed and repeated those words aloud, "God is a God of reconciliation." I made the decision, I was going to move to West Virginia. Kurtis and I moved forward with the reconciliation, five months after reconciling we were engaged, five months after reconciling we were re-married. Our second ceremony was intimate and informal. Only close family and friends were invited and the ceremony was performed by Pastor Brett.

Unchained

I grew up witnessing people close to me love each other then resent each other. When drugs or alcohol came into play, they would hate each other. I remember walking along the river bank and thinking to myself that I wanted something different. I did not how to get that something different. I felt chained to the life that I witnessed but determined not to follow in those footsteps.

Even though, I was raped as a virgin at the age of seventeen and was a survivor of domestic violence, I would continue on the path to earn my higher education. I would continue to pursue goals that were out of my league because I knew with hard work, determination, perseverance, and a tenacious spirit any dream that I wanted could be obtained. NFL Cheerleader, actor, respected fitness entrepreneur, and a professional bodybuilding bikini competitor are only a few accolades.

I think the most important thing I have learned on my journey is to take the lessons learned from those around me and make my life better. One of the reasons I probably became resentful is because maybe I saw a glimpse of me in the people that surrounded me growing up and I wanted to run away. I wanted to bury that part of me. It was only by my pain and suffering that I could understand and have compassion for their pain.

My first failed marriage taught me to be true to myself in the pursuit of achieving my goals but remain grounded enough to not move across the country. I needed to allow my child the opportunity to know and have a close relationship with his father.

My second marriage has taught me about the importance of keeping the family together. It was up to Kurtis and I to protect our family and keep it together. The depression and isolation that I experienced while being divorced from Kurtis, allowed me to think about my mother's pain. I was used as an instrumental person in her life and we both have talked about it and come to terms with it. I am proud that my mother and father are living addiction free lives and both will turn seventy years old this year.

I consider myself a woman unchained because I refuse to become a victim of the obstacles and challenges which I may be presented. When presented with challenges, I will discover how I am going to overcome it. I will unleash my faith and apply positive action to keep my life moving forward in the direction of purpose. I want every goal that I aspire to be achieved and I believe all my goals will come to fruition.

I have learned that a woman unchained walks with her head held high, she embodies self-worth, she does not allow self-pity to stop her from achievements, she takes care of others but she does not become so overwhelmed in taking caring of others that she forgets about her own needs. Co-dependency weakens, but self-worth strengthens. I have achieved most of my goals because of being determined. My future goals will be achieved because I know to embrace self-worth and determination. Self-worth and determination are the twin forces that I will hold onto to achieve new goals and dreams. I am a woman unchained!

Redskin Cheerleader Pictures

WASHINGTON REDSKINS CHEERLEADERS

Weigthloss Transformation Pictures

Fitness Pictures

Love

A Woman Unchained

About the Author